"What Tommy has captured so beautifu[...] Philippians 4:8 serves to get joyless, criti[...] This book reminds us all that we have a [...] to our thought life and that right choices [...] Prepare to be challenged! If you want rev[...] ...inking, then read this book!"

JANET PARSHALL
Nationally syndicated talk show host

"Tommy Newberry's book is a surefire primer for finding authentic joy in the center of God's will. And thank the Lord, Tommy is honoring God by writing books like this one."

DON PIPER
New York Times bestselling author of *90 Minutes in Heaven*

"*The 4:8 Principle* is one of only a small handful of books that have deeply influenced me over the last decade. I have shared it with many friends and thousands of youth leaders across the country. In this book, Tommy Newberry amplifies his call for joy and shows us, step-by-step, how to activate 4:8 throughout our lives. Read this book and spread the joy!"

DR. JEANNE MAYO
President of Youth Leader's Coach; youth communicator; author

"If we desire more joy, then we need to line up our thinking with the apostle Paul's advice in Philippians 4:8. Tommy coaches us to put this powerful principle into practice! With this book, you'll be inspired to leave your comfort zone behind and start living in the joy zone."

BRYANT WRIGHT
Senior pastor of Johnson Ferry Baptist Church; president of the Southern Baptist Convention

"This book is a powerful and practical resource. It is a must-read for anyone interested in improving their quality of life and their relationship with God."

GREGORY A. DALE, PHD
Professor of sport psychology and sport ethics at Duke University; author of *It's a Mental Thing!*

"Simple, relevant, and powerful, the 4:8 message continues to touch lives in deep and meaningful ways. If you want to live each day with more joy, then read this book."

JEREMIE KUBICEK
CEO of GiANT Impact; author of *Making Your Leadership Come Alive*

"Straight to the point and fun to read, this book will inspire you to think differently about . . . everything! Read this book and feel the joy."

JON GORDON
Bestselling author of *The Energy Bus* and *The Seed*

"If you want to experience a joy-filled life, I challenge you to not only read but put into practice the wisdom in this book. Tommy has a way of provoking, challenging, and inspiring that has transformed my life as a husband, a father, and a pastor. I hope you experience the same journey."

JEFF MULLEN
Lead pastor at Point of Grace Church

"In less than six weeks, Tommy Newberry will change your life from the inside out. In a world where we measure transformation in years, this book is literally a Godsend."

TIM SANDERS
Bestselling author of *Today We Are Rich*

"In this book, Tommy Newberry makes experiencing joy simple and achievable for everyone. Follow Tommy's game plan—live the 4:8 Principle for forty days—and you'll be amazed at the transformation . . . and so will everyone around you!"

GREG L. JANTZ, PHD
Author of *Battles Men Face*

"This book shows you how to guide, guard, and gauge your thoughts every day. Tommy communicates convincingly that if we can harness what goes on in our minds, joy can be the norm in our lives; the rule, not the exception."

DR. TIM ELMORE
President of GrowingLeaders.com; author of *Nurturing the Leader within Your Child*

"This is a book for serious people—for Christians who hunger for 'something more' and are willing to exert effort to fulfill that yearning."

CECIL MURPHEY
Coauthor of *90 Minutes in Heaven*

"In this book, Tommy Newberry lays out a plan for making joy an everyday experience. Timeless truths mixed with real-life examples make this book fun to read and highly practical."

EVA PIPER
Author of *A Walk in the Dark*

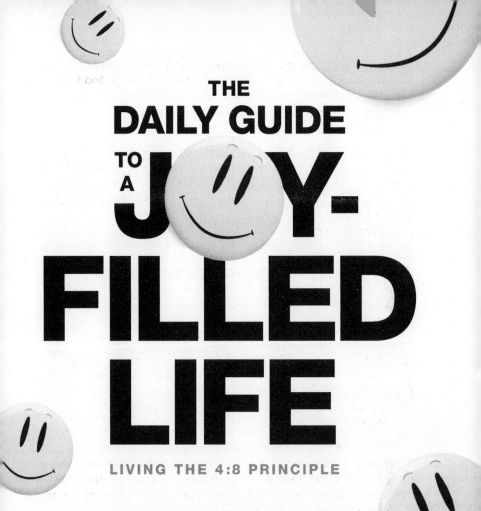

THE
DAILY GUIDE
TO A JOY-
FILLED
LIFE

LIVING THE 4:8 PRINCIPLE

TOMMY
NEWBERRY

TYNDALE
MOMENTUM®

The Tyndale nonfiction imprint

Visit Tyndale online at tyndale.com.

Visit Tyndale Momentum online at tyndalemomentum.com.

TYNDALE, Tyndale's quill logo, *Tyndale Momentum*, and the Tyndale Momentum logo are registered trademarks of Tyndale House Ministries. Tyndale Momentum is the nonfiction imprint of Tyndale House Publishers, Carol Stream, Illinois.

The 1% Club, Success Is Not an Accident, and *America's Success Coach* are registered trademarks of The 1% Club. All rights reserved.

The Daily Guide to a Joy-Filled Life: Living the 4:8 Principle

Copyright © 2012 by Tommy Newberry. All rights reserved.

Previously published in 2012 as *40 Days to a Joy-Filled Life: Living the 4:8 Principle* under ISBN 978-1-4143-6690-6.

Published in association with the literary agency of The Knight Agency, 570 East Ave., Madison, GA 30650.

Smiley face photograph copyright © Nicholas Eveleigh. All rights reserved.

Author photo by Ted Domohowski copyright © 2009. All rights reserved.

Designed by Jennifer Ghionzoli and Dean H. Renninger

Scripture quotations marked NLT are taken from the *Holy Bible*, New Living Translation, copyright © 1996, 2004, 2007 by Tyndale House Foundation. Used by permission of Tyndale House Publishers, Carol Stream, Illinois 60188. All rights reserved.

Scripture quotations marked NKJV are taken from the New King James Version.® Copyright © 1982 by Thomas Nelson. Used by permission. All rights reserved.

Scripture quotations marked NIV are taken from the Holy Bible, *New International Version,*® *NIV.*® Copyright © 1973, 1978, 1984, 2011 by Biblica, Inc.® Used by permission. All rights reserved worldwide.

Scripture quotations marked KJV are taken from the *Holy Bible*, King James Version.

Scripture quotations marked *The Message* are taken from *THE MESSAGE,* copyright © 1993, 2002, 2018 by Eugene H. Peterson. Used by permission of NavPress. All rights reserved. Represented by Tyndale House Publishers.

Scripture quotations marked AMP are taken from the *Amplified Bible,*® copyright © 1954, 1958, 1962, 1964, 1965, 1987 by The Lockman Foundation. Used by permission.

For information about special discounts for bulk purchases, please contact Tyndale House Publishers at csresponse@tyndale.com, or call 1-855-277-9400.

ISBN 978-1-4964-5071-5

Printed in the United States of America

27	26	25	24	23	22	21
7	6	5	4	3	2	1

*This book is dedicated with gratitude to all
those who bring joy to the world.*

Table of Contents

Acknowledgments

The book you are reading reflects the hard work and creativity of many people!

Thank you to my agent, Pamela Harty, and to Carol Traver at Tyndale, who believed in this particular project and helped make it happen. Big thanks to Karin Buursma for meticulously examining every word in the manuscript and challenging me to communicate my message in the most effective way possible.

I am grateful for "The 4:8 Launch Team," who mobilized in unison to expose *The 4:8 Principle* to thousands and thousands of important relationships five years ago. The team includes Jim Wade, Scott Goodman, Dave Armento, Sean Boyd, Ron Raitz, Matt Levin, John Seckman, Mike Ivey, Kyle Jenks, Dale Lewis, Bradley Fulkerson, Denny Summers, Randy Leeder, Mike Campbell, Cathy LaMon, Quill Healey, Ken Ashley, Ed Easterlin, Palmer Bayless, Joe Hamilton, Bruce Carlisle, Jeff DeHart, Tom Elias, Ware Bush, Jason Bilotti, Ryan Cone, Chad Wade, Steve Owings, Clay Rolader, Matt Hawkins, Shane Benson, John Patterson, Jim Barber, Gil Harvard, Sid Johnson, Clay Gilbert, Judy Crawford, Sharp Gillespy, Clark Gillespy, Frank Lyles, Duncan Gibbs, Mark Kemp, Charles Wellborn, Mark Seeley, Hal Grayson, John McIntyre, Darin Wiggins, Joel Benson, Todd Thompson, Mark Riley, Bert Clark, Charlie Bello, Ben Stephens,

Bo Jackson, Bruce Boring, Cindy Martin, Suzanne Murphy, Jenny Griscom, and Beth Irvin.

Because of your efforts, thousands of lives have been positively blessed with the joy of 4:8 Thinking. Notes and e-mails filled with stories of transformed relationships and renewed attitudes flow into our office daily. You made this happen. And without your help spreading the 4:8 Message, this sequel would not be possible. Thank you.

Thanks to Jeanne Mayo, Ginger Herring, Curt Beavers, Mark Crawford, Lisa Thrift, and Lars Dunbar for repeatedly sharing *The 4:8 Principle* with your best relationships. Thanks to Bill Orender, Mark Marchesani, and Jim Kocher for exposing *The 4:8 Principle* to Primerica. Thanks to Hunter Hill, Chaplain Mike Shannon, and Operation Gratitude for sharing *The 4:8 Principle* with the US Armed Forces overseas. Thanks to Chandra Adams for sharing *The 4:8 Principle* within the prison system.

Thanks to Randy Gilbert, Rick Frishman, and David Hancock for your counsel. I appreciate your advice, encouragement, and tactical expertise. Thanks to Robert Truelove, Shelly Guberman, and Hudson Phillips for what you do behind the scenes that helps me be better at what I do.

I am especially grateful to my assistant, Becky Kirkman, who encouraged me to sit down and write while she kept the business running and distractions out of sight.

Eternal thanks to my parents, whose unconditional love and encouragement continue to have a positive influence on my day-to-day life. Continuous thanks to my wife, Kristin, who joyfully tolerated the many late evenings and long weekends of writing.

Foremost, I want to thank God for the opportunity and inspiration to write about the things that matter most.

Introduction:
I Should Have Had a 4:8

WHEN I WAS A TEENAGER, my grandmother shared with me a certain Bible verse that grabbed my attention and provoked my interest. Over the years that followed, I kept this verse in front of me and often contemplated its meaning as I experienced my own life unfolding. As I launched my coaching practice in 1991, I began sharing this special verse with clients, curious whether it would touch and challenge them as deeply as it had me.

As time passed, I observed, first with individuals and then with couples and families, that this single passage from the New Testament contained within it the secret to a joy-filled life. By applying this verse to their daily lives, my clients started amplifying the joy they experienced in their marriages, with their parenting, and in their lives as a whole.

Of course, the verse I am referring to is Philippians 4:8:

Whatever things are true, whatever things are noble, whatever things are just, whatever things are pure, whatever things are lovely, whatever things are of good report, if there is any virtue and if there is anything praiseworthy—meditate on these things. (NKJV)

Today, we live in a culture inundated with negative headlines that spread images of despair and defeat around the globe in a matter of seconds. Wars continue. Children starve. Tragedy strikes. Corruption abounds. Families break. Scandals erupt. Debt grows. Storms rage.

As a result, we have become far too comfortable accepting the unacceptable and viewing the world, our lives, and ourselves in a defeatist way that directly competes with the passionate, joy-filled, and faith-driven people God desires us to be.

Many years ago, I was listening to a missionary speak at a fund-raiser for YWAM when she raised the question she feared many others were quietly contemplating: "With so many bad things going on in the world, how could there be a God?"

My impulsive response, which I blurted out, surprised me and caught the speaker off guard: "With so many good things going on in the world, how could there *not* be a God?"

I believe it was that very moment, inspired by God and nurtured by my grandmother Lilli, that eventually led me to write *The 4:8 Principle* ten years later, and it continues to fuel my motivation to coach readers with this book.

Based on Philippians 4:8, the 4:8 Principle states that whatever you give your attention to expands in your experience. If you dwell on your strengths, your blessings, your goals, and all the people who love you, then you will attract even more blessings, even more love, and even more accomplishments. It's a powerful truth. While trials and tribulations are permanent fixtures of this world, our attitudes toward them can help soothe the wounds and bring about solutions while glorifying our heavenly Father in the process.

In this book, I will show you how you can be the catalyst for "stubborn joy" throughout your life. But be forewarned:

clearly, this is not a book about thinking the way most people think. Rather, this is a book about thinking the way *few* people think. If you are okay with being a part of this joyful minority, we can work together to transform it into the majority!

But first things first. Start with yourself. Allow this book to challenge your edges, awaken your faith, and nudge you away from the junk that limits your joy.

Throughout the pages that follow, I will coach you to think, speak, and act in a manner that will bring about the abundant joy of life that God had in mind when he first envisioned your existence. Being full of joy doesn't mean that your life is perfect. It means that you trust that God has good plans for your life, no matter what is happening right now! It's an outward sign of inward faith in God's promises.

This book has been written to help you put the 4:8 Principle into practice in your everyday life . . . *for the rest of your life*. Even sporadically using the 4:8 Principle will bring about worthwhile results. But the rewards of wholeheartedly living the 4:8 Principle are immense and more than worth the prerequisite effort. That is what this initiative is all about. Think of this forty-day exercise as Operation Activate 4:8. When you sincerely activate the 4:8 Principle in your life, it will become a defining moment for your spiritual growth and personal development. You will never turn back.

The process this book follows is near and dear to my heart. As a life coach for over twenty years, I have specialized in helping my clients reach and exceed their goals. The best results have always followed repeated exposure to the right principles over a reasonable period of time. In my experience, forty days is an appropriate time frame for making definite progress with a principle that will bless you and your loved ones indefinitely.

Of course, a quick glimpse through the Bible reminds us of the special spiritual significance to the forty-day time frame as well. We know that Noah's transformation came through forty days of rain, Moses spent forty days on Mount Sinai receiving the law, and of course Jesus had perhaps his deepest spiritual experience withstanding forty days of temptation in the desert.

If you have already read *The 4:8 Principle: The Secret to a Joy-Filled Life*, you will love the reinforcement and the action-oriented approach of this book. Better still, you will build rapid momentum as a result of your preexisting appreciation of this principle. Think of it as your *joymentum*!

If you have not yet read the original 4:8, you will find the book you are holding to be a user-friendly way to become fluent with a life-enhancing principle. And I am confident that once you have completed this boot camp for joy, you will be inspired to grab a copy of the original!

The key distinction between this book and its predecessor is the obvious emphasis in the sequel on activating this attitude. This is not a trivial difference. As human beings we often *know what to do*, but we frequently do not *do what we know*. This book has been organized to overcome this particular feature of our human nature.

When you put this book aside at the end of Day 40, you will not be magically free of trouble and tragedy, but you will be equipped to process the world, including the desperate times and difficult people, in a way that multiplies your joy and the joy of those with whom you are investing your life.

Turn to the next page to find out how to get the most from this book. Let's get started!

How to Use This Book

Game Plan from Coach

I HAVE DESIGNED forty consecutive life lessons that each highlight a key component of the 4:8 frame of mind. Studying the 4:8 Principle in these brief, easily digestible chunks helps you assimilate the ideas and take ownership of the message. You will find that each of the forty chapters, or days, supplies you with an important concept to meditate on for the rest of the day, further helping you incorporate the 4:8 Perspective into your unique mental makeup.

Make this book an active read. Highlight passages that stand out or seem to be speaking directly to you. Make notes in the margin when you read an idea that is particularly relevant to your circumstances. Paraphrase inspiring thoughts in your own words. Make the 4:8 Message *your message* to the world!

Following each lesson or meditation, you will find an "Activate 4:8" drill followed by an "Extra Mile" assignment. These exercises are drawn from mental drills that I have used for more than two decades in my private coaching practice. They are intended to sharpen your thinking, illuminate blind spots, and discipline your mind so that you are ready to experience maximum joy. Investing the time and thought power to do these exercises will pay huge dividends for both you and your closest relationships.

Next, you will find a "Make It Stick: Thought of the Day," which is intended to help you stay aware of the 4:8 Principle as you go about your normal daily routine. Consider texting or e-mailing it to yourself after you finish the chapter so you'll have a handy reminder with you at all times. For example, I have set a recurring alarm on my iPhone that reminds me every day at precisely 4:08 p.m. to "Think 4:8."

Finally, each chapter concludes with a brief prayer thanking God for his goodness and inviting his direction as you attempt to live with more joy.

There is nothing to gain from rushing through this book. Please work through the chapters one day at a time so you will experience the full impact of the day's lesson and have the opportunity to contemplate what it all means to you and your most important relationships.

Please read through this book in sequence the first time around. Along the way, I encourage you to reread those special chapters that seem to be speaking directly to you. When possible, reread these chapters aloud for double reinforcement.

Finally, consider making the journey through this book an annual ritual, like spring training for your mental and emotional fitness. Just as the best baseball players in the world return to the basics before each new season begins, I encourage you to revisit the fundamentals of joyful living at least as often.

Your Joy Blesses Others!
Coach

THINK THIS, NOT THAT

The Joy of Free Will

A HEALTHY BODY produces energy. Likewise, a healthy mind produces joy. This is not an accident. If you want to experience vibrant health and abundant energy, it is essential that you consume certain foods and drinks and refrain from consuming others. The same is true if you want to lose weight or put more muscle on your frame. You have to say yes to the foods that lead you toward your goal and no to those that lead you away. Very simply, you need to eat this, not that. And while, for the most part, this is now considered common sense, it is not always common practice for those desiring to reshape their physical bodies or increase their energy levels.

Progress toward joy begins the same way, with a firm decision to cut back on *joy-reducing* thoughts and increase *joy-producing* thoughts. In short, you have to change your mental diet. You have to *think this, not that*. After all, joy is the sum and substance of emotional health.

Many well-meaning individuals desire to be leaner or more energetic but then continue to indulge in a diet and lifestyle that takes them in the opposite direction. Consequently, they do not reach their goal. Many with the goal of increased joy run into the same predicament: they keep consuming a mental diet mismatched with their goal. In both instances, there is a major disconnect between desired objectives and daily behavior.

Joy is a state of mind that must be purposely cultivated if you are to live and love and influence others as God intended. Fortunately, joy does not depend on the outer conditions of your material life, but rather on the inner condition of your mental life. Joy is the result of something strikingly simple, though not necessarily easy: *consistently thinking joy-producing thoughts.*

Is this within your grasp? Is it even possible for anyone to accomplish? Before you answer, let me remind you that few endeavors worth pursuing come easily to anyone, and the attainment of a joy-filled spirit is no exception. There are risks in shooting for this gold standard of faith in action. There is a high price to be paid, and it must be paid in advance. Certain comfort thoughts will need to be relinquished. Counterproductive habits will need to be abandoned. Tenured excuses must be surrendered.

Since you are free to choose what you think about, and you have billions of options, what specific thoughts should you increase to become joy filled? What specific thoughts should you decrease? What kinds of thoughts will distress your soul? What types of thoughts will nourish and hydrate your soul?

At any given moment we can consciously choose to

- think excellent thoughts, not mediocre thoughts;
- think focused thoughts, not scattered thoughts;
- think fresh, exciting thoughts, not stale, boring thoughts;

- think compassionate thoughts, not harsh thoughts;
- think innovative thoughts, not common thoughts;
- think loving thoughts, not indifferent thoughts;
- think energetic thoughts, not exhausted thoughts;
- think constructive thoughts, not destructive thoughts;
- think helpful thoughts, not hurtful thoughts;
- think successful thoughts, not failure thoughts;
- think faith thoughts, not fear thoughts;
- think fit thoughts, not fat thoughts;
- think bold thoughts, not comfort thoughts;
- think opportunity thoughts, not security thoughts;
- think giving thoughts, not getting thoughts;
- think serving thoughts, not self-centered thoughts;
- think grateful thoughts, not entitled thoughts;
- think abundant thoughts, not lacking thoughts;
- think responsible thoughts, not irresponsible thoughts;
- think reconciliation thoughts, not retaliation thoughts;
- think principled thoughts, not popular thoughts;
- think positive thoughts, not negative thoughts;
- think thoughts of victory, not thoughts of defeat; or
- think about the promises of God, not the problems of this world.

Think about what you want, not what you don't want. Why is this required for joy-filled living? Very simply stated, we tend to bring about what we think about. As King Solomon counseled, "As [a person] thinks in his heart, so is he" (Proverbs 23:7, NKJV).

Building on Solomon's wisdom, James Allen wrote that "the outer world of circumstance shapes itself to the inner world of thought, and both pleasant and unpleasant external conditions are factors which make for the ultimate good of the individual. As the reaper of his own harvest, man learns both by suffering and bliss."[1]

It is my intention that during this forty-day regimen, you will start experiencing more of the bliss that is called joy-filled living. Starting today, release the need to hang on to thoughts that haven't worked well for you.

It is true that we can think this, not that!

ACTIVATE 4:8 ::::::::::::::::::::::::::::

Drill #1

Think about the person you intend to become. Then on the following page, identify a few specific thoughts that are incompatible (Not That column) with that vision. In the left-hand column, identify a handful of thoughts that are compatible (Think This column) and helpful. At the bottom, write a short sentence indicating your commitment to improve your thinking.

The Extra Mile

Invite a trusted friend to participate with you over the next forty days. Send a brief e-mail to each other before midnight every day sharing what you deem the most valuable concept or "aha moment" from that day's lesson. If possible, talk about the experience once per week by phone or over a cup of coffee.

THINK THIS

NOT THAT

Make It Stick: Thought of the Day

I am free
to choose my
thoughts.

Prayer

Heavenly Father, thank you for the freedom to select my thoughts. Today, nudge me to think the right thoughts all day long. Amen.

DEAL OR NO DEAL

The Joy of Decisiveness

DO YOU BELIEVE that God has great plans for your future? I often ask my audiences this question, and predictably they respond by unanimously raising their hands in affirmation. Of course, they know the answer I am looking for, so it is probably not a very reliable test.

Besides, I am not asking the question for theoretical reasons. I want to know: if God himself were in your presence in physical form and directly affirmed his great plans for you, what would be different about the way you would live from that point forward? Would anything change?

Do you believe that God has grand plans for your future? Stop reading, and make sure you have answered this question truthfully. If you answered no, then skip the rest of this chapter and move on to Day 3.

Since you are still reading, I know that you either answered yes or you are simply blowing off my instructions. Assuming you answered yes, do you really believe it? Do you believe it intellectually or do you believe it in your heart, with every fiber of your being? If you accept that God has a great future planned for you (see Jeremiah 29:11), then this belief must naturally translate into behavior that is consistent with that belief.

Who, when assured of a wonderful future, would sulk, complain, and mentally escape with hours of excessive television and other distractions? Often we act today as though tomorrow does not hold much promise. However, I believe that once you accept that God's will for you is something amazingly great, it alters the way you behave and interact in some dramatic, obvious, and observable ways. You will begin to respond with gratitude. Do you agree?

In the popular TV game show hosted by Howie Mandel, there's always a moment when the catchphrase is spoken: "Deal or No Deal?" This is the moment of truth. Will the contestant take the money offered by the "banker" or, instead, choose to bet on the unknown amount of cash in the briefcase? This is the best part of the show. With the cameras rolling and the pressure building, the contestant has to make a decision.

I love the phrase "Deal or No Deal" because it forces the contestant to get out of the neutral zone and take a stand. It's exciting to see whether the decision ends up being a good one or a bad one. But when it comes to choosing to believe that God has good plans for us, we rarely have someone standing over us insisting that we make a decision. The same is true with choosing gratitude, the cornerstone of 4:8 Living. Consequently, it is too easy to perpetually postpone this life-altering decision. With no cameras rolling and no host prompting us, we freeze, we stall, and we rationalize, but we do not respond to the call of "Deal or No Deal." Instead, we linger in the land of "Wait and See," effectively deactivating one of the greatest faith builders and joy amplifiers available to us.

Gratitude is a *choice*. It is a conscious and deliberate decision to focus on life's blessings rather than its shortcomings. Life will always have shortcomings, and it will always have virtues. When you focus on your blessings, your life feels abundant. When you focus on what's missing, life feels incomplete. Where you point the spotlight of your attention is purely a matter of choice.

The power of gratitude is undeniably immense. Without a doubt, a perpetual spirit of thankfulness is the central ingredient in the recipe for a joy-filled life. You are going to draw more joy out of your business, out of your marriage, out of your family life, and out of all the other aspects of your existence when you make a commitment to become an openly and overtly grateful person.

Gratitude is also an effective antidote to most negative emotions. You cannot experience gratitude and hostility at the same time; you have to make a choice. Which one is it going to be? The more things you appreciate today, the more things you will notice tomorrow to be grateful for. On the flip side, the less appreciative you are today, the fewer blessings you will tend to acknowledge tomorrow. The Greek philosopher Epictetus said, "He is a wise man who does not grieve for the things which he has not but rejoices for those which he has."

Today's focus is the conscious decision that precedes this thankful state of mind. My challenge to you is to take a stand and make this decision—right now.

What are you going to do?

Own your joy! Either make the decision to be an exceptionally grateful individual from this point forward, or make the decision *not to be*. Life's camera is rolling, and now is the time to make a choice. Decide to decide. This is the moment of truth. Are you ready to take a leap of joy? Is it Deal or No Deal?

ACTIVATE 4:8 :::::::::::::::::::::::::::::::

Drill #2

Using bullet points, describe what God's plan for your life might look like.

- _____

- _____

- _____

- _____

- _____

- _____

- _____

- _____

- _____

- _____

- _____

- _____

The Extra Mile

Write a brief note to God, thanking him for the amazing future he has planned for you. Give thanks for the joy you gain from pondering this mysterious future. Ask God to reveal the next most important steps you should take to bring about his will for your life.

_____

_____

_____

_____

_____

_____

_____

_____

_____

_____

_____

_____

_____

_____

Make It Stick: Thought of the Day

I am ready
to take a
leap of joy!

Prayer

Father God, thank you for the amazing future you have planned for me. Today, help my heart to overflow with gratitude as I reflect upon those awesome plans. Amen.

HUNDREDS OF PROBLEMS, MILLIONS OF BLESSINGS

The Joy of Perspective

MINDFUL OF THE 4:8 PRINCIPLE, my wife, Kristin, and I often joke that we each have ten positive qualities and ten not-so-positive traits. She is certainly giving me the benefit of the doubt in this regard! But despite our best efforts at overcoming this ratio, it is unlikely to change very much. Thirty years down the road when we are celebrating our fiftieth wedding anniversary, I will still have my positives and negatives, and so will she.

No doubt those positives and negatives may shift around a bit as we grow spiritually, experience more of life together, and acquire a deeper appreciation for each other. Nonetheless, both of us will remain imperfect. Our relationship will be both good and bad.

What really matters is what we choose to focus on as individuals within our marriage. If Kristin chooses to focus on what's lacking in me, she's going to experience a deficient husband. If I choose to focus on what is missing in Kristin, I'm going to experience an incomplete wife. The quality of our relationship will depend on whether we are mature enough and faithful enough to focus on what is *beautiful, excellent, and worthy of praise* in each other.

As I grew up, I was taught that life was going to have its good times and its bad times. There would be the inevitable ups and downs. This advice made sense to me. What I didn't realize when I was young, however, was that both the ups and the downs were going to be happening all the time.

Your neighborhood is a mixture of good and bad. Our nation is a mixture of good and bad. Marriage is a mixture of good and bad. Parenting is a mixture of good and bad. This life is, in fact, a mixture of both positive things and negative things.

The basis for the 4:8 Principle is the advice of the apostle Paul as recorded in Philippians 4:8, where he challenges us to seek out and dwell on the positives in our lives:

> Whatsoever things are true, whatsoever things are honest, whatsoever things are just, whatsoever things are pure, whatsoever things are lovely, whatsoever things are of good report; if there be any virtue, and if there be any praise, think on these things. (Philippians 4:8, KJV)

In my workshops, for emphasis I display the last segment of Philippians 4:8 as rendered in the Amplified Bible:

> If there is any virtue and excellence, if there is anything worthy of praise, think on and weigh and take account of these things [fix your minds on them].

I also share the translation from *The Message*:

Summing it all up, friends, I'd say you'll do best by
filling your minds and meditating on things true, noble,
reputable, authentic, compelling, gracious—the best,
not the worst; the beautiful, not the ugly; things to
praise, not things to curse.

Consider this verse carefully for a moment. The very fact
that Paul is telling us what we should focus on reveals a critical point:

We always have a choice.

If we didn't, this verse would be unnecessary. If we were
naturally positive all the time, Paul wouldn't emphasize this point
so dramatically. If we could not control our negativity, this teaching would be in vain, unrealistic, and beyond our capability.

Paul is reminding us that *we have a choice.* With God's help,
we can control our thoughts. Further, his words teach us that
the choice is between good and bad, between excellence and
mediocrity. Life is never completely good or completely bad.
There will always be some junk, and there will always be some
greatness.

Your marriage, your health, and your finances may be in
outstanding condition, but you might be facing learning difficulties with one of your children. Maybe your kids are all thriving,
but your marriage remains stuck in a frustrating chapter of
the relationship. Or perhaps your family life is wonderful, but
you're disappointed with your circle of friends, your weight,
your faith, or the condition of your home.

You will always have something to complain about, and you will always have some blessings to count. Inevitably, life is filled with peaks and valleys. But even in the valleys, there will always be something working really well in your life, and even on the mountain peaks, not everything will be perfect. Life is always a mixture of good and bad.

Think about watching the evening news. Even though lots of great, positive things are going on in the world, almost everything the television news highlights is terrible stuff that has, unfortunately, already happened. Arguably, there is not a lot to gain from watching it, unless it deepens your understanding of important events or prompts you to pray and take productive action.

It is definitely worth evaluating the quantity of bad news that you currently ingest. Even weather reports slant toward the negative. Imagine hearing "There's a 70 percent chance of sunshine tomorrow" instead of "There's a 30 percent chance of rain." You'd probably fall out of your chair!

Leading with the negative is how the news is delivered, but it doesn't have to be how you run your life. Even though there will always be cloudy days, you don't have to make blemishes the essence of your life. Leave that for the news reporters. That is their job, not yours.

You have hundreds of problems and millions of blessings! Whether you choose to count your blessings or complain about what is wrong with your life, recognize that *you do have a choice.*

Life is always a mixture of good and bad.

ACTIVATE 4:8 :::::::::::::::::::::::::::::

Drill #3

To really appreciate the lopsided ratio of blessings to problems, make a list of both in the space indicated below. In the left-hand column, identify your current problems. Don't hold back. Include everything you deem to be a real issue for you. In the right-hand column, identify your blessings—everything you are glad to have or glad *not* to have in your life. Then, at the bottom, identify a few blessings you expect to be grateful for in the future.

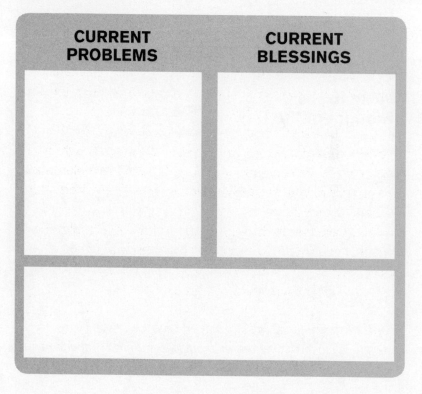

CURRENT PROBLEMS	CURRENT BLESSINGS

The Extra Mile

Paraphrase Philippians 4:8, customizing the verse to fit your life. Insert your name and those of your family and friends. In your own words, make this passage specific to your particular world of relationships, strengths, challenges, opportunities, and goals for the future.

_____

_____

_____

_____

_____

Make It Stick:
Thought of the Day

I see the blessings that surround me.

Prayer

Lord, thank you for all my blessings and even all my problems. Help me this day to think in a way that multiplies the good stuff and minimizes the bad stuff. Amen.

THE FIFTEEN-MINUTE MIRACLE

The Joy of Daily Solitude

A JOY-FILLED LIFE is the result of joyous decades, joyous years, joyous months, joyous weeks, and joyous days. But you can live a joy-filled life only one day at a time. Therefore, to boost your potential for joy, start with the essential daily foundation. After all, if you take care of the days, the decades will take care of themselves.

If you're going to "seek first the kingdom of God," as we're taught in Matthew 6:33 (NKJV), then doesn't it make good sense to schedule an appointment with your Creator first thing in the morning? When your first meeting of the day is with your heavenly Father, your day is established upon the rock of his truth. Could there be a more important appointment all day long?

Visit with your heavenly Father before you visit with anyone else—and before you have turned your attention to the demands of the day. The early morning hours are ideally suited for prayer, meditation, and Bible study, as well as personal reflection and course correction. It is upon awakening in the morning that your mind is most peaceful and receptive to insight and inspiration. Quality thinking is far less likely in the agitated or cluttered mental state that often follows a hectic day of work.

Be still, and remind yourself that God is in control. Take time every single day to resurrender every corner of your life to him. Contemplate the size and scope of God. Remind yourself that any problem is small when compared to your heavenly Father. Experience the cleansing, renewing, and invigorating power that is always available to you.

Program your mind to produce a joy-filled day by saturating your mind with Scripture, following your prayer routine, and then reviewing your personal mission statement, goals, and daily priorities. Whatever you do, pour God into your morning before you expose yourself to the headlines and heartaches of the day.

There is no better example of living on purpose and putting first things first than making this morning meeting with God a nonnegotiable daily priority. If you're seeking joy, it's okay to skip a meal or even skip a workout, but never cheat yourself of the calm, quiet confidence that comes from this rock-solid start to your day. I have found that when I feel like I can least afford to invest this time, that is precisely when I need it the most.

Since God created you and the universe, why not let him help you create your day? Think about it. If you had access to the smartest person in your field and she offered to mentor you every morning, would you accept that invitation? If you had an entrée to the wisest human being alive today and he offered to coach you each day, would you accept that offer? Of course you would!

With God, though, you have far more than you can even humanly imagine. Because he is all-powerful, he can help you with anything. And because he knows everything, you can go to him with all your questions and concerns. Since he has infinite wisdom about your business ventures and family dynamics, this opportunity is simply too good to pass up.

Investing this time first thing in the morning is a single discipline, but it carries with it multiple spiritual rewards, including joy, insight, renewal, and peace of mind. Additionally, you'll move on with the rest of your day with the confident assurance that you have, for today, sought first the Kingdom of God.

It's time for a quick checkup!

How do *you* currently start the day? Do the first fifteen minutes of your morning glorify God and set the foundation for a joy-filled day? What do you feed yourself mentally and spiritually after awaking? I have witnessed more positive progress from helping my clients fine-tune their early morning routines than from any other single lifestyle adjustment. What you do first thing in the morning sets the emotional tone for the entire rest of the day. If your morning doesn't start with joy, you will find it difficult to catch up later.

First thing in the morning, before your mind gets entangled with the busyness and obligations of the day, is the perfect time to work on your "Joy Software." Upload your gratitude and then download God's grace. Invite God to reveal what he wants to see happen in your life today. Ask him about that next most important step he wants you to take. If necessary, wake up fifteen minutes early to seize this opportunity. Before long, you will find yourself positively addicted to this Early Morning Joy Ritual (EMJR), and you will never want to start your day any other way.

Fifteen minutes has proven to be long enough to make a palpable difference and still short enough to inspire busy folks to give it a try. If you're ever tempted to say that you don't have time for this solitude with God, ask yourself bluntly, "What could I possibly do with that time that would bring me any greater benefit?" Minutes invested in praying for wisdom will save days spent in overcoming mistakes.

If you invest just fifteen minutes each morning in preparation for joy, it will add up to seven-and-a-half hours in the first thirty days alone and approximately ninety hours in a year. This is the Fifteen-Minute Miracle.

ACTIVATE 4:8 :::::::::::::::::::::::::::

Drill #4

Create your Fifteen-Minute Miracle. Reference the following questions for ideas. Then, on page 24, identify the four key elements in your Early Morning Joy Ritual (EMJR).

1. What could I read, watch, or listen to during the first fifteen minutes I'm awake?
2. What should I avoid reading, watching, or listening to?
3. How could I prepare myself for this EMJR the night before?
4. What could I tell myself the instant I wake up every morning?
5. What should I avoid telling myself the instant I wake up?
6. How could I intensify my gratitude in the First Fifteen?

7. How could I use prayer and Scripture?
8. How could I use the 4:8 Questions?
   (See Day 23 for more detail.)

The Extra Mile

To decrease the chances that your EMJR will be put off, get organized the night before. Decide on a distraction-proof location. Itemize your agenda. Prepare the coffee. Gather together your Bible, devotional, 4:8 Questions, books, music, journal, and anything else you may need to connect with God, and kick the day off to a joyful start.

Make It Stick: Thought of the Day

I joyfully launch each day with God!

Prayer

Lord, I am grateful for the serenity found most abundantly in the early morning. Help me every day to meet first with you before I face the rest of the world. Amen.

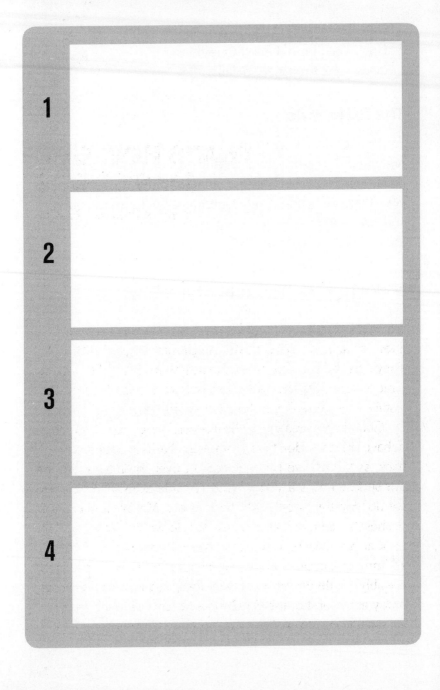

THAT'S HOW GOD MADE DOGS

The Joy of Prudent Thinking

WE HAVE A DOG named Gracie. When she starts barking, guess what happens with the neighbors' dogs? That's right! They start barking. And when the neighbors' dogs start barking, Gracie barks right back. This is an instinct, I suppose—a factory-installed response. That's how God made dogs.

God did not create us to be like this. Nevertheless, we often behave like dogs, don't we? Somebody barks at us and we bark back, as though we have no control over the matter. Maybe our spouse tosses a verbal hand grenade at us, and what do we do? We throw one right back at her. Maybe our teenager pushes that certain button, and what do we do? We push right back at him. Maybe it is a coworker who sets us off, initiating an immature cycle of impulsive replies that leave us distracted, possibly a little embarrassed, and most certainly with a deficit of joy at the end of the day. It doesn't have to be this way.

I recently jumped the gun at a four-way stop near my

youngest son's school, going before it was my turn. As I
pulled through the intersection, I mouthed "Sorry" and raised
my hand to the driver I had cut off, trying to acknowledge
my mistake. He returned my apologetic gesture with a rude
gesture of his own, along with a demonic expression. As he
drove behind me for several miles, he continued to "salute
me" enthusiastically as he spotted me glancing in the rearview
mirror.

It doesn't have to be this way.

In today's lesson, I want to highlight two types of thinking. The first is *reactive*. The reactive thinker is much like the
offended driver, unwilling to control his automatic negative
reactions. This type of thinking requires no effort at all. The
second type of thinking is *proactive*, and this does require
some set-up time.

If you are a reactive thinker, no prep work is required.
You just show up and react to your circumstances in whatever
manner comes naturally to you. In some circumstances, things
work out fine. In other situations, not so much. When you are a
proactive thinker, however, you have to think ahead. You have
to be intentional and consider your responses ahead of time,
outside the heat of the moment.

As a proactive thinker, you decide that no matter what is
going on around you, you are not going to allow it to change
what is going on inside you. You tell yourself things like this:

- "I keep my thoughts lined up with God's promises
  for me."
- "Despite how others treat me, I am going to treat them
  with respect and kindness."
- "My joyful heart is revealed most in stressful situations."

- "With God's help, I remain poised and calm, even in negative conditions."

When we overreact to what other people do, we are living outside of what God wants for us. I do not believe God ever intended for us to delegate control of our emotional life, and we do ourselves no favors when we hand over that control to others.

At a recent planning retreat, I talked to married couples about this commonly uttered phrase: "You make me so mad." As we talked, we exposed this expression for the ruse it is. The truth is that no one can make you mad without your permission. In other words, it is not what someone else does that triggers your negative response. Rather, it is how you interpret what others say or do that unleashes your darker emotions.

Often, though, we give people in our lives consent to make us angry. Strangely, we tend to do this with our family members and others who are closest to us. It is sort of funny to consider, but the people we love the most are the ones who can "make us the maddest." Do you recall my encounter with the gentleman at the four-way stop? He didn't even know me, much less love me. What do you think he is like at home?

To surrender control of your emotional life to other people, whether to loved ones or to strangers, means certain forfeiture of your potential for joy. When I realized that God never intended for other people to have that much power over whether I am having an up or a down day, it quickly became an added incentive for me to keep my emotions in check. What about you?

ACTIVATE 4:8

Drill #5

Becoming a proactive thinker requires thinking ahead. Today's drill moves you in that direction. Consider three recurring negative or stressful situations you face. Write these in the space on the following page, along with three potential responses. The first response is *poor (8:4—the opposite of 4:8)*, the second is *acceptable*, and the third is *optimal (4:8)*.

The Extra Mile

Today, pray and ask God for the self-control to respond to difficult people and situations in a way that glorifies him. Then place a physical reminder, such as a sticky note or 3 x 5 card, in a location where you will see it often, such as on your laptop, bathroom mirror, or steering wheel. On the reminder, write the phrase, "With God's help, I am a proactive thinker!"

Make It Stick: Thought of the Day

I am a proactive thinker, and it shows!

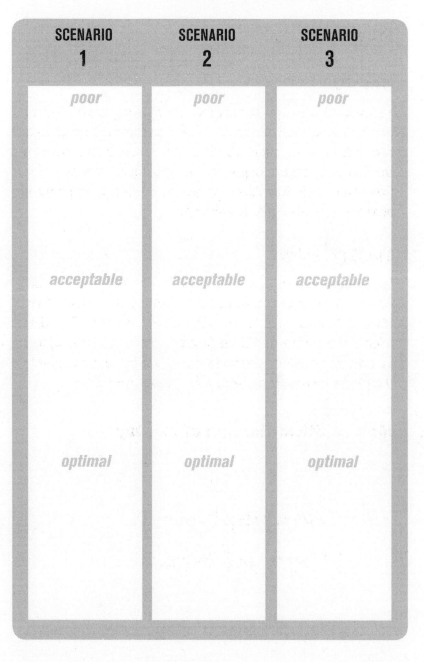

SCENARIO 1	SCENARIO 2	SCENARIO 3
poor	*poor*	*poor*
acceptable	*acceptable*	*acceptable*
optimal	*optimal*	*optimal*

Prayer

God, thanks for how you made dogs and how you made me. Today, help me to be proactive with my thoughts so that I glorify you with my emotions. Amen.

WRITE YOUR OWN HEADLINES

The Joy of Goals

ENOUGH OF THE NEGATIVE news stories already.

Steer clear of the defective thinking that the media indulges in. Instead, break from the pack and chart your own course. Starting today, write your own life story and make the headlines sensational!

Your written goals are your headlines for the future. Make them captivating, and you'll rise above and beyond your previous best . . . and breathe in much more joy all along the way. Goals work because we all enjoy *moving toward* something we want to experience. That's why it feels so much better to head off on a long-overdue vacation with family and friends than it does to endure the long car ride home. Goals give us a tangible target as we move forward in life.

Develop goals to grow your faith as well as your finances. Develop goals to become a better spouse and a stronger parent. Develop a goal to become fit and maybe even a goal to have more fun. I encourage you to carve out a block of time and create "back to back to back" goals so that you will have an uninterrupted agenda of family adventures, personal achievements, and other etched memories to look forward to and *move toward* for at least the next decade.

Goal setting is one of the most powerful tools for cultivating a 4:8 mind-set and living the joy-filled life. Unfortunately, it is also extremely underutilized. Parents abdicate the teaching of this skill to the schools. Schools omit it from the curriculum. Churches breeze over the subject entirely. And the barrage of burning items on our to-do lists keeps many adults scattered and frantic, simply winging it through their entire lives, never knowing there was an alternative approach. It doesn't have to be this way.

Goals tell your brain what to notice in the midst of a crowded thought life. Imagine a football stadium packed full of fans wearing light gray sweatshirts . . . all except for ten daring young men who have painted their entire torsos bright red. Bold, precise goals stand out in your mind like those guys stand out to the videographer in the blimp flying overhead.

Goal setting is an essential tool for disciplining your mind to focus on what is lovely, excellent, and worthy of praise. Your goals reveal what you want to see come true in your life. In addition, the presence of clearly written goals equips you with a physical mechanism for focusing your attention on the good stuff, making it far easier to be a faithful steward of your mind.

Your goals will reflect the elements of your life that are worthy of affection, reflection, and meditation. Philippians 4:8 doesn't only teach us to think deeply about overtly spiritual things, such as the nature of God, what heaven will be like, or what we love and respect about our spouse. Instead, Paul's advice contains a particular word that is worth considering: *whatever.*

Whatever is true.
Whatever is noble.
Whatever is right.
Whatever is pure.
Whatever is lovely.
Whatever is admirable. (NIV)

I may not know you personally, but I predict that most of your goals could be described with one or more of the words above. Assuming I am right, can you see how establishing goals and then dwelling on them will simultaneously move your life forward and keep you in the joy zone? (Please note that *whatever* is not used in Philippians 4:8 in the same manner as many teenagers use it to reply to a parental request!)

Those without written goals and the focus they provide waste undue mental energy thinking about the wrong things. The "wrong things" may include their fears, doubts, and inse- curities, as well as their grievances against specific people or the world at large. Neglecting to select and formalize goals puts you at risk of becoming an upside-down 8:4 Thinker con- sumed with critical thought patterns. While it may be possible to maximize your potential for joy without goals, it places a pointless handicap on the entire pursuit.

A joy-producing goal is a written commitment to create an outcome that is fixed, measurable, time bound, and com- patible with God's Word. Pursuing goals forces you to grow and become more like the person God wants you to become. Goals simplify decision making and help you delay gratifica- tion. Also, becoming goal directed builds your character and disciplines you to say yes to the right things and no to the wrong things.

With clear goals, you make important decisions in advance—thus avoiding the natural human tendency to drift into the world's agenda. Goals elevate you from remorse to legitimate change and improvement. They are proof that you are serious about your God-given potential and your God-given responsibilities. Goal setting is simply harnessing your strengths to make a positive difference in the world. So get with God and lobby for some huge goals. After all, with one person committed to a goal, God can transform the world. He's done this many times and will doubtless do it again.

Noah's goal was to obey God by building a boat. Moses' goal was the exodus of his people. David's goal was to kill the giant Goliath. Jesus' goal was to give his life as a ransom so that others may have the opportunity to live more abundantly. Paul's goal was to carry God's Word to the unsaved. Aren't you glad these key biblical figures were single minded and focused on their goals? An entire theme from Genesis to Revelation is that God has goals for his people and that he accomplishes goals through the lives of his people. Even the physical Bible itself is dynamic evidence of a written goal. God himself put down his goals in writing for our benefit.

What about you? Are you ready to set some huge goals?

A thirty-five-year-old husband and father of two young children began praying to God for strength and power to reach his very ordinary goals, but as time passed, the power did not come. One day the father, in a bit of frustration, asked God, "Why haven't you answered my prayer?" God replied simply, "With goals no bigger than yours, you don't need my power." Set goals so huge that when you reach them, you'll be certain that God helped you!

An unwritten goal has no power, energy, or authority in

your life. Write it down and make it happen! God plus goals plus you is an unbeatable combination.

ACTIVATE 4:8 :::::::::::::::::::::::::::

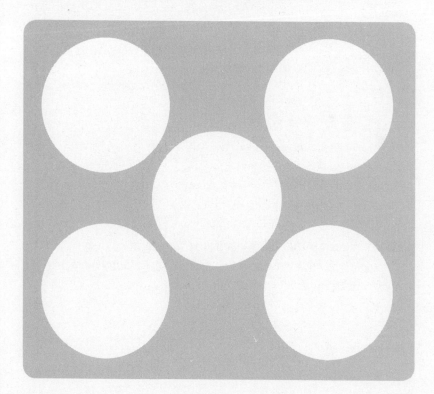

Drill #6

In the space indicated below, brainstorm some of the goals you might want to achieve before your life is over. I call this SDIMJWT (Someday I Might Just Want To).

The Extra Mile

In light of your lifetime goals, what are some of the smaller goals you might want to accomplish in the next forty days? Consider faith, relationships, family, fitness, and finances. Be encouraged; a lot of joyful momentum can be created in just forty days!

Make It Stick: Thought of the Day

> I am goal directed
> and having
> a blast!

Prayer

Lord, thanks for the gift of goals and for the things you want to accomplish through my life. Today, help me to keep my mind on my goals and off my fears and worries. Amen.

FOCUS CREATES FEELING

The Joy of Awareness

WE BECOME what we behold.

At any given moment, you can choose to pay attention to what's present or what's missing, what's working or what's broken, what you achieved or what you messed up, what's available or what's unavailable, what's possible or what's impossible, and what excites you or what frightens you. And, in so doing, you will win or lose the battle for your mind.

In a nutshell, whatever you dwell upon becomes increasingly conspicuous in your own mind. That's the principle of attention, something I have branded as the 4:8 Principle to accurately reflect its scriptural origin.

Here's how it works: the more you emphasize your good health with both your silent thoughts and your public speech, the healthier you feel. The more you stay mindful of the positive qualities in your spouse, the closer and stronger your relationship will become. The more attention you give your kids, the more influence you will have in their lives. The more you mull over God's promises, the greater your spiritual convictions will become.

Alternatively, the more you mentally replay a particular injustice, the more frustrated you will become. If you constantly replay mental movies of what is broken, you will notice more of what is broken.

If your emotional life today is not where you ultimately want it to be, then your top priority should be shifting your attention to your blessings, to your strengths, and to the aspects of your life that are working. Resist the urge to accelerate negative emotional spirals by chronically reporting your own negative headlines. Stop talking so much about your mistakes, setbacks, and disappointments. There is no way around this principle of thought. You *will* experience a deficit of joy when you allocate a surplus of attention to the things that dissatisfy you.

Refuse to fuel negative emotions by constantly talking about what is wrong with your marriage, your youngest child, your sore back, your peculiar neighbors, and the world in general. Instead, broadcast your blessings to anyone who will listen. Verbalize your vision for the future to trusted friends and allies. Turn the spotlight of your concentration to your future hopes and dreams, to the grand and mysterious future that God has in store for you. Your emotional life can advance only after your negative thoughts retreat.

Although most people are not automatically positive, neither are we hopelessly negative. Our lives tend to imitate the thoughts that we entertain most consistently. The clear corollary of this is that we feel what we dwell upon. Our focus determines our feelings. This is the power of the 4:8 Principle.

We condition our minds to value what we read, watch, study, discuss, and ponder. What absorbs our interests shapes how we think. Whatever holds our attention molds our intention. What we contemplate, we internalize. What we internalize, we emotionalize. The more frequently we think about something, the tighter the grip it exerts on us, the decisions we make, and the actions we take. Whatever we idolize shapes our character.

The thoughts you think most often reproduce in your mind. You will always feel what you focus on. Naturally, the flip side of the 4:8 Principle is that whatever you ignore, or cease thinking about, begins to fade away. If you have too much of something in your life, this prescription is for you. If you have too much negativity, fix your mind on your blessings. Starve worry, fear, and doubt by no longer nourishing them with your attention.

Accept that your focus brings about your feelings. If you have an urge to "go negative," remember that doing so cannot produce anything positive.

ACTIVATE 4:8

Drill #7

On the following page, write down up to four ways you intend to upgrade your thought life in order to upgrade your emotional life. If you prefer, simply identify four productive thoughts you intend to think more frequently.

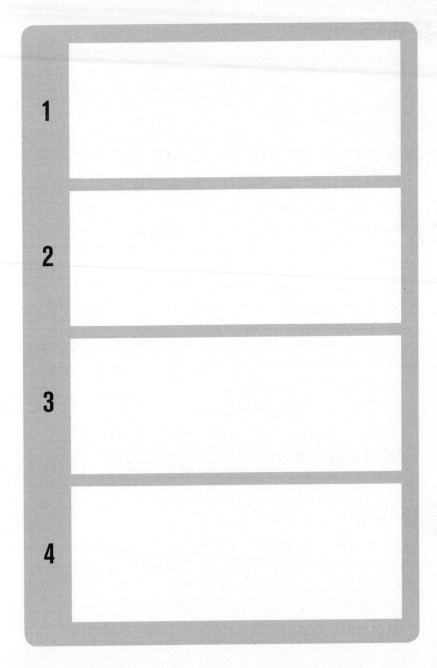

The Extra Mile

Ensure that you are focusing on the good stuff. As each day progresses, record its positive occurrences and joyous moments for later reflection. Shoot for at least four daily positives. If you prefer, reflect upon your day at bedtime and jot down the progress made and other good news from that day. Total time required is four minutes or less, but the joyful effect adds up quickly.

Make It Stick: Thought of the Day

My focus creates my feeling!

Prayer

Heavenly Father, thank you for the freedom to select my thoughts. Inspire me today to think thoughts that reinforce the wonderful future you have planned for me. Amen.

STOP IDENTITY THEFT

The Joy of Knowing Whose You Are

YOU ARE A BEAUTIFUL, wonderful child of God!

When you view yourself in the positive light of scriptural truth, you will have a much easier time experiencing a joy-filled life. Unfortunately, many people lose sight of their true identity and consequently miss out on the joy God intended for them. It doesn't have to be this way. Understanding how your self-concept influences your attitude toward life can help you both live with and spread more joy.

Your self-concept is the picture that you hold of yourself at the unconscious level. It forms gradually throughout your life and generally includes the beliefs you have about the past, present, and future. While you cannot touch it or see it, your self-concept is operating behind the scenes, 24-7, for better or for worse. The future portion of your self-concept, often referred to as the *self-ideal*, projects an internal image of antici-pated future success and satisfaction (or lack thereof). Based primarily on your interactions with others, your *self-image* promotes its version of who you are today. And your *self-worth*, the third component of the self-concept, reflects how valuable you consider yourself to be outside of tangible achievements.

The words and images that float through your mind when you are judging yourself flow from your self-concept. While you are not consciously aware of whether this composite picture is helpful or hurtful, the thoughts you think, the words you speak, and the actions you take all get their operating instructions from your self-concept.

The good news is that you were not born with a self-concept. The self-concept you possess today is the net result of your exposures, both good and bad, over your entire lifetime. Given the culture we live in, it takes a deliberate and persistent effort to create and maintain a healthy, productive, and joy-producing self-concept. In today's lesson, we'll discuss how to upgrade your self-concept. To a large degree, applying all the other lessons in this book will also contribute to an accurate and joyful identity.

Here's a key point: *Your true self-worth is based only on what God says about you, not on how you feel about yourself.* If you owned the original of a famous painting but believed it to be only a copy, would that errant belief determine the painting's actual value? It might accidentally define the sale price, but the fact that you underestimated the value based on erroneous information wouldn't change the value of the artwork. The true value of the painting is based on whether the art is an original or a copy.

Likewise, you are an original masterpiece, handcrafted by the Creator of the universe. In fact, the Bible uses these exact words to describe us! "We are God's masterpiece. He has created us anew in Christ Jesus, so we can do the good things he planned for us long ago" (Ephesians 2:10, NLT). Whether or not you understand it, your true value is based on what God says about you, not on what you do or how you feel about yourself.

The Bible reveals these truths about each of us:

- You are important. (See 1 Peter 2:9.)
- You are forgiven. (See Psalm 103:12.)
- You are a new creation. (See 2 Corinthians 5:17.)
- You are protected. (See Psalm 121:3.)
- You are family. (See Ephesians 2:19.)
- You are strong. (See Psalm 68:35.)
- You are unique. (See Psalm 139:13.)
- You were created for a purpose. (See Jeremiah 29:11.)
- You are victorious. (See 1 John 5:3-5.)

There has never been and never will be anyone just like you, and God has not made anyone else in the world out of better clay than he used to make you. Your life here on earth is your special, unrepeatable opportunity to fulfill God's vision for your life and to magnify the joy he has placed within you.

Do you see yourself as a child of almighty God? Remember *whose* you really are. You are an original masterpiece. Recognize that the true you is not your flesh and bones. You are a spiritual being living a temporary human experience—a dress rehearsal for eternity. A mediocre self-concept does not come from God but from the blemishes and stains of the world. It comes from seeing ourselves differently than God sees us. It comes from disagreeing with God. It comes from continuing to identify with the things that haven't worked. It comes from continuing to think about ourselves as unworthy, as if we've forgotten about the blood of Jesus Christ that cleanses and purifies us. *This certainly violates the 4:8 Principle.*

When you remind yourself of your true identity, you will find it much easier to live according to Philippians 4:8 and filter out the junk that steals your joy. Likewise, when you practice the 4:8 Principle, it is far easier to accept yourself as a kid of the King. When you see yourself as a child of God, you do not accept artificial restrictions on the quantity of joy or the level of impact you can have in this world. That's critical because how you perceive yourself sets the ceiling for what God can do with you.

When you see yourself as down and defeated, that is what you will surely be. This woeful approach does you no good personally and only serves to minimize your contribution in the world. However, if you choose to see yourself as more than a conqueror through Christ (see Romans 8:37), you will certainly ascend to that level.

And the world tends to accept you at your own valuation.

ACTIVATE 4:8 :::::::::::::::::::::::::::::::

Drill #8

Write three bold statements that reflect what you believe it means to be a beautiful, wonderful child of God.

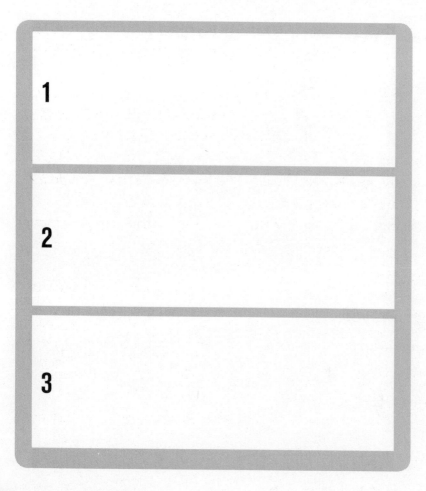

1

2

3

The Extra Mile

Rewrite the verses shared in today's lesson on sticky notes and display them around your home. Place the verses at the bottom of e-mails to friends and family. Dig through the Bible and find additional validation for your true identity. Make sure your kids know whose they really are and why!

Make It Stick: Thought of the Day

I am someone
worth dying for!

Prayer

Father, how awesome it is that I am a beautiful, wonderful child of God! Today, remind me whose I really am and keep me from discounting myself with my thoughts and speech. Amen.

TAKE A VACATION
FROM YOURSELF

The Joy of Shaking It Up

FROM TIME TO TIME, it's a wise idea to schedule some special rejuvenation just for you. Once you have been revitalized, you can expect to feel invigorated, full of joy, and ready to face the challenges of this world with divine passion.

While it certainly makes good sense to take some regularly scheduled vacations and trips with your family and friends, have you ever contemplated what it might be like to escape from yourself, even just for a few days? I know this is a peculiar question, but you have to admit this experiment might be sort of fun, right? You can't get out of your body, of course, but you can hit the "refresh" button on your mind, creating a mental vacation that updates your perspective, reloads your enthusiasm, and rebuilds your potential for joy.

You can accomplish this mental getaway by varying some of your habits, especially your thought patterns, for a week or so. Stale, stagnant thoughts can fill our thinking so gradually that we hardly notice the stealthy effects on our attitude. It doesn't have to be this way. During this unconventional "vacation," make an extra effort to drop all brands of negativity, including the more subtle ones. Cut out criticizing and condemning others, especially your spouse, kids, and coworkers. Knock off any kind of gossip or grumbling about other people.

Refrain from exasperated mannerisms or facial expressions that divulge frustration or annoyance—even if they are seemingly justified. Refuse to discuss your aches, pains, and old wounds with friends and family. If you can't resist these kinds of conversations, spare your loved ones and find a stranger with whom you can discuss these matters. Temporarily suspend worrisome thoughts and speech. At a minimum, postpone these self-defeating habits until you "return home." Think of this as healthy, joy-producing procrastination.

Are you still looking forward to this vacation? Or are you already getting homesick?

During this inspiring and invigorating getaway, your objective will be to think, speak, and act in a manner consistent with the 4:8 Principle. Keep your mind as well as your mouth preoccupied with what is beautiful, excellent, true, just, and worthy of praise. Pray and forgive beyond the norm for you, whatever that may be.

Verbally encourage your spouse, friends, family, and coworkers. Defend the target of gossip. Predict positive outcomes aloud. Review your blessings, especially the little ones. Smile more. Laugh more. Think and review your goals. Use spare moments to dwell on the character of God.

In this secret and idyllic "vacation spot," you will notice that the people and situations in your life appear to be different because, as Thoreau wrote, "we find only the world we look for."[2] You will be looking for—and consequently finding—fresh value in your relationships and circumstances, and new virtue within yourself.

After all, it's easy to get so consumed with your obstacles that you forget about your goals. It is easy to entertain hostile thoughts about the future and end up missing the gift of the present. This is not for you!

Once you're in a better place mentally, why not shake up the rest of your routine? If you normally read a lot in the evenings, try watching a little TV instead. And if you typically watch TV each night, give it up for a week and just read. If you hardly ever read fiction, then find a classic novel and dig into it. In the morning, read a different newspaper, or maybe take a week off from the news altogether. Visit some new websites or pick up a magazine you've been interested in.

Enjoy some food that's unusual for you, and shop for it at a different grocery store. Take an alternative route to your office in the morning, and pay attention to the new sights along the way. Avoid the usual exercise routine. If you typically run, then try walking. Or try exercising during lunch, for a longer period of time, or with a partner if you normally work out solo.

Visit some friends you haven't seen much lately, or make an effort to initiate a new friendship. Shake up your spiritual life as well. Worship at a new church, or try praying in a different way. Consider rereading your favorite inspirational classic, that one book that positively shook up your faith. Maybe you could mix in some fresh spiritual disciplines or simply substitute some new rituals in lieu of your normal routine. Could you initiate more time with joy-filled friends or maybe carve out a chunk of uninterrupted time with your Creator?

These are just a few ways to "stir the pot" and create a vacation from yourself. I'm sure you can devise many more.

You can always "return home" from this brief vacation, but you might just find you like it too much to come back.

ACTIVATE 4:8

Drill #9

What would you do differently if you "took a vacation from yourself"? On the following page, list up to four conditions of this getaway or changes you would make during this vacation.

The Extra Mile

Recruit a friend to join you on this unique escape. Pick a mutual start date for your getaway and share your experiences with each other along the way. Consider journaling, blogging, or even posting your observations on Facebook.

Make It Stick: Thought of the Day

> I am rut free
> and rejuvenated!

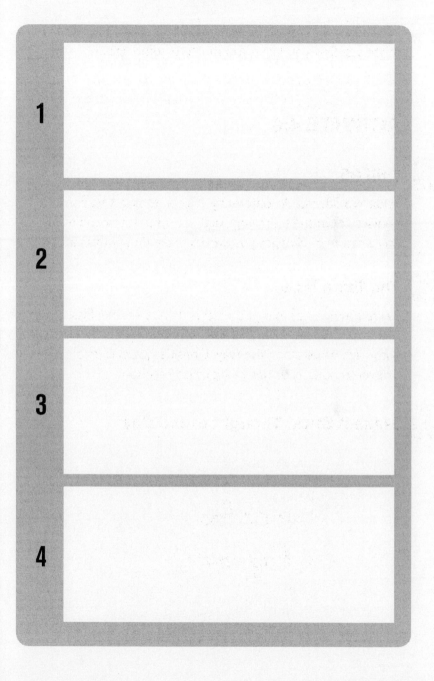

Prayer

Lord, thank you for new ideas and the blessing of variety that is available to each of us. Dislodge me today from that which is stale, and invigorate me with something bold and fresh in your creation. Amen.

THE SECRET STUDIO

The Joy of Creation

THE SECRET TO LIVING an exceptional life *tomorrow* is thinking strong, joyful thoughts *today*. Living exceptionally is the net result of feeding your mind with the kind of high-quality ideas and limitless possibilities that will set you free and allow you to thrive as God intends.

The invisible battle you wage against your human nature will be won or lost in the mind. Minute by minute, hour by hour, in the hidden workshop of your mind, you are constructing thoughts of good or evil, joy or depression, success or failure. You are writing your own life story with each subtle thought you think.

Almost everything that happens to you, good or bad, originates with a single thought. Neuroscientists can now demonstrate that every thought sends electrical and chemical signals throughout your brain, ultimately affecting each cell in your body. Thoughts can influence your sleep, your digestion, your pulse, the chemical makeup of your blood, and all other bodily functions.

The truth is, the top-secret conversations you hold in the privacy of your own mind do not stay confidential forever. These thoughts will eventually be revealed for everyone to see. A dream, a business, or a marriage dies first in the mind. Your best and worst decisions began with an individual thought.

What you persistently think sooner or later crystallizes into the words you speak, then the things you do, and ultimately, the circumstances you help bring about. Today, remind yourself that "your thoughts are showing." More than that, your thoughts are incrementally shaping your destiny here on earth.

With every thought that races through your mind, you are reinventing yourself and your future. Research indicates that the average person thinks approximately fifty thousand thoughts per day. This is really good news . . . if you think really good thoughts. Naturally, it's bad news if you think bad thoughts. Every thought steers you either toward your God-given potential and abundant joy or away from it. You are never "on the fence" or "in the neutral zone" with your thinking. Every individual thought matters.

Unfortunately, roughly 90 percent of the thoughts you have today are reruns from yesterday and the day before. These ingrained thoughts produce predictable results. This is the chief reason why most people tend to resist positive change. Comfortably cemented thoughts simply carry more clout than good intentions, and consequently, the status quo maintains an impressive winning streak.

If your aim is to maximize your potential for joy, you must first discipline yourself mentally. This is your responsibility, and you must immediately take ownership. Then God can honor your faith and empower you to live a life of excellence. Make the shift from random, reactive thinking to deliberate, purpose-driven thinking. Think the thoughts you would think if you wholeheartedly trusted God's promises. Refuse to become bent out of shape with everyday inconveniences, delays, and disappointments. Turn your mountains into molehills by discussing God more than your difficulties. Assume the good intentions of others. Maintain the mood that corresponds with answered prayers.

You have authority over your thoughts, but God will not force you to exercise this aspect of your free will any more than he will compel you to exercise regularly, eat a healthy diet, read the Bible, or wear your seat belt. Right thinking is a choice you have to make for yourself. If you are intentional and persistent, you can select your thoughts and in so doing shape your life here on earth into something spectacular. The alternative is to give up this sovereignty and instead live a life of mediocrity dominated by uncertainty and suspense. *It doesn't have to be this way.*

In Romans 12:2, we are taught that transformation is the result of a renewed mind. The apostle Paul writes, "Do not conform to the pattern of this world, but be transformed by the renewing of your mind. Then you will be able to test and approve what God's will is—his good, pleasing and perfect will" (NIV). This means improvement is preceded by improved thinking. More joy follows *more* joyful thinking. First allow God to retrain your thoughts and feelings, *and then* experience God's best for your life.

Many people conform to the trends of this world. Too often, people struggle to remake their circumstances (health, marriage, finances, addictions), when they should be asking God to help them remake their minds. Once our minds are renewed, conditions often take care of themselves.

ACTIVATE 4:8 :::::::::::::::::::::::::::::

Drill #10

In the space below, write up to eight positive affirmations that reflect the kind of person you are determined to become, all beginning with the words *I am*.

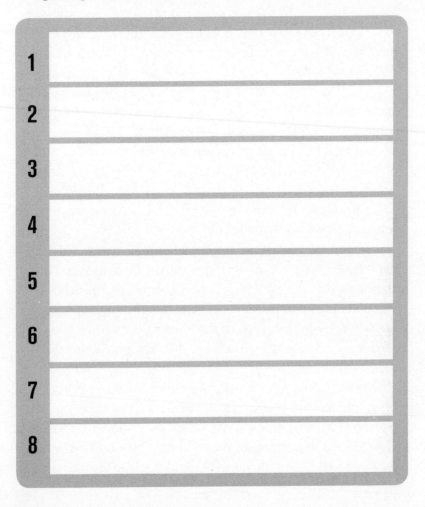

The Extra Mile

When we think like everybody else, we become like everybody else. To avoid this conformity, elevate your thought life. To kick off this process, brainstorm at least eight ways you could renew your mind and improve your thinking over the next forty days.

1
2
3
4
5
6
7
8

Make It Stick: Thought of the Day

My thoughts are showing!

Prayer

Heavenly Father, thank you for giving me authority over my thoughts. Bless me today with a renewed mind and the positive transformation that naturally follows. Amen.

HARBORING GRATITUDE

The Joy of Appreciation

GRATITUDE RELEASES JOY.

Gratitude is a magnetic force that naturally draws joy-filled people and occurrences into your life. When you experience a sense of gratitude, it means that you have been harboring thoughts of appreciation for the abundance in your life. When you feel a sense of deficiency, on the other hand, it does not necessarily mean that you are lacking something important. What it does mean is that you have recently been thinking about what is *absent*, very likely to the exclusion of what is *present*.

You might have been thinking about your spouse's annoying quirks and overlooking all the reasons you married him in the first place. You might have been thinking about being under financial pressure and forgetting that you have just about everything money can't buy.

Gratitude is like a mental gearshift that takes you from

turbulence to peacefulness, from stagnation to creativity. Gratitude brings you back to the present moment, to all that is working well in your life right now. Gratitude predisposes your heart to joy, and it is the cornerstone of an unstoppable attitude. Exceptional gratitude is the practice of relentless praise and thanksgiving. And I am glad to report that this is not something you're born with. We can at least be thankful for that, right?

Gratitude can be learned and cultivated throughout your lifetime. To facilitate this intentional development, it is helpful to view gratitude in three distinct ways.

First, *gratitude is a choice*. It is a conscious and deliberate decision to focus on life's blessings rather than its shortcomings. When you focus on your blessings, your life feels abundant. When you focus on what's missing, life feels incomplete. Next, *gratitude is a feeling*. It is a sense of joy and appreciation in response to receiving a gift, whether that is a concrete object or an abstract gesture. Finally, *gratitude is also a capacity*. It is the learned skill of creating value in routine situations and relationships.

On Election Day 2006, one of my good friends and long-time clients, Bo Jackson, lost his son, Parker, in a freak, one-car crash near his home in Milton, Georgia. Several months later, Bo sat down with me and shared how he was coping with Parker's death. To illustrate, Bo took a piece of notebook paper and sketched a simple diagram. At the top of the page he wrote *God*. Underneath, from left to right, he wrote the words *grief, grace,* and *gratitude*. At the very bottom of the page, he wrote *goodness*.

Pointing to the drawing, Bo explained that while there was nothing good about the accident, God's presence in their midst brought great comfort to him and his wife, Lauren, as they grieved. Clearly, God's grace was sufficient, even in these extraordinary circumstances. But as Bo related, the peace they felt as parents fluctuated depending on whether or not they actively practiced gratitude, as awkward and unnatural as that felt at the time.

Wrenching as it was, when Bo and Lauren consciously thanked God for the sixteen years they had with Parker, as opposed to thinking about all they would miss in future years as a result of his death, they experienced God's grace and peace at remarkable levels. When they dwelled on Parker's salvation and that of the other teenagers who came to Christ as a result of his accident, they felt the Lord's goodness flowing through them. Amplified by the right focus and grounded in God's promises, it was an amazing demonstration of faith.

As a result of today's lesson, I want you to become hypersensitive to the power of gratitude in helping you live a strong and joy-filled life. I'm confident you recognize that gratitude is vital to a life of joy. But are you expressing that appreciation consistently with your thoughts, words, and actions? Would your friends, family, and coworkers agree with you?

Do you stand out as an unusually grateful person? Our hectic, often overloaded modern culture can easily distract us from following through on our good intentions. It is easier than ever to take our blessings for granted. How grateful do you think you are?

Take a moment to evaluate yourself using these questions:

- What is positive and distinctive about your family?
- What are three of your best memories from your first year with your spouse?

- How has gratitude enabled you to experience God's grace, even in the midst of a trial?
- What is the most interesting goal you have already accomplished?
- What parts of your body tend to work really well most of the time?
- In what ways has God shown his grace in your life recently?
- What is the nicest compliment you have received in the last thirty days?
- What is the most valuable lesson you have learned from another person?
- What is the most beautiful thing you've seen or heard in the last week?
- What is a rough situation from the past that in retrospect has turned into a blessing or benefited you in some way?
- What is the number one thing you are going to be grateful for this time next year?

How did you do? If you're fostering an attitude of gratitude, the answers to most of these questions will probably come readily, because you'll be used to thinking positively about circumstances in your life. Have you appropriately given thanks to God for the blessings that surround you? Do the people you love the most know how grateful you are for them? People who live by the 4:8 Principle don't necessarily have more in their lives to be grateful for; they just give more attention to their blessings than to their difficulties.

What about you?

ACTIVATE 4:8 ::::::::::::::::::::::::::::::::

Drill #11

Give some consideration to your four most cherished blessings and write them below on the left. To the right, identify how you consistently show thanks with your thoughts, words, and actions. Would your friends, family, and coworkers agree with you?

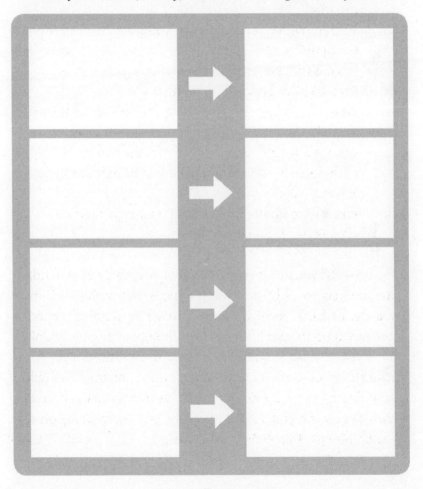

The Extra Mile

Enjoy forty-eight-second gratitude shots throughout the day. Set the alarm on your phone or watch as a reminder. When the alarm goes off, pause to think about the multitude of things in your life that are currently working well. Offer a brief prayer of thanks for your loved ones, customers, or coworkers. Shoot a one sentence thank-you text to your spouse. Contemplate the positive aspects of the day so far. Congratulate yourself for the progress you have made in the last hour or two.

Make It Stick: Thought of the Day

I am an unusually grateful person.

Prayer

Heavenly Father, thank you for the priceless feeling of abundance that comes from actively practicing gratitude. Today, alert me to the people whom I can bless with my overt appreciation and thankfulness. Amen.

4:8 YOUR MATE!

The Joy of Marriage

MARRIAGE IS GOOD and bad.

This is not breaking news! Every husband and every wife are imperfect, both gifted and flawed in numerous, often unpredictable ways. Consequently, nowhere is the apostle Paul's advice from Philippians 4:8 more valuable, more practical, or more enduring than in the arena of marriage.

In life, and especially in relationships, there will always be some junk that accompanies the joy. Just consider the complexity of permanently merging two very different human beings together, no strings attached! This is all part of God's plan. He designed marriage to reflect divine love, meaning that just as he "loved us first" (1 John 4:19, NLT), we are to love our mate *first*, even when he or she is not acting quite so loving. In fact, if we love our spouses only when they are treating us well, can it really be labeled love at all?

In the famous "love passage" read at many weddings, Paul describes true love in this way:

Love is patient, love is kind. It does not envy, it does
not boast, it is not proud. It does not dishonor others,
it is not self-seeking, it is not easily angered, it keeps
no record of wrongs. Love does not delight in evil but
rejoices with the truth. It always protects, always trusts,
always hopes, always perseveres. Love never fails.
(1 Corinthians 13:4-8, NIV)

That's a high standard indeed. But the way that we actually
implement this high standard of love is by following the instructions of Philippians 4:8. First Corinthians defines love. Philippians
shows us the mental path to demonstrating such love.

Consider that every thought you think about your spouse
either strengthens or weakens the foundation of the relationship. Thoughts about your husband are not neutral. Thoughts
about your wife are not neutral. Every thought matters. Warm,
caring thoughts build up; cold, selfish thoughts tear down.

Thinking critically about your spouse, even if you believe
it is warranted, will postpone true intimacy and the closeness
you both desire. As relentlessly as you may try, you cannot
think one thing about your mate and experience something
different in the relationship.

Much of the negative thinking about your spouse occurs
when he or she is not around. Nonetheless, the effects of this
"invisible" negativity will, in due course, become visible in your
common space as a couple.

No one on the planet has such a dominating influence on
your self-worth as your mate. In fact, in a marriage there is
a collective self-image that establishes a ceiling of fulfillment
and satisfaction for both of you. In other words, as a husband
builds up his wife, he builds up the whole relationship. As a

wife affirms her husband, she is affirming the future she really desires. This is important to keep in mind 365 days a year. Since you are doing this life together as one, why not do it right, with gratitude, grace, and greatness?

Marriage, like the rest of life, is never all good or all bad. Inevitably, permanent relationships are filled with peaks and valleys. But even in the valleys, not everything will be rotten. There will still be some things worth appreciating. And even on the mountain peaks, stresses and struggles will certainly linger. Not everything will be perfect. Could it be that the pressures of marriage have more to do with how God wants us to grow spiritually than how happy he wants us to become?

I have the privilege of frequently speaking alongside clinical psychologist Dr. Mark Crawford. He reminds audiences over and over again that "soul mates are created, not discovered." He elaborates on this countercultural warning by teaching, "The idea of finding your soul mate is a myth. A soul mate is created by sharing the best and worst experiences of life together over a period of many, many years."

It is easy to see how misunderstanding this concept could lead to all sorts of false assumptions about the natural tensions between two people committed to each other for life. Sadly, instead of looking for the single reason to adhere to their wedding vows, couples often nonchalantly ruminate on all the reasons to abandon their promises to each other, as though this were an acceptable exception to the rule outlined in the fine print somewhere.

Many husbands and wives justify withholding positive attention from each other because they don't happen to feel like giving it. Unfortunately, these feelings can quickly cement into emotional habits that act like an emergency brake on the quality of the relationship. People squander positive energy in seeking material evidence to validate their rotten feelings. And since all spouses disappoint each other, evidence to confirm the discontent is always available.

But by now you know that these rotten feelings are not accidental. They flow naturally from the animated thoughts that stubbornly fuel them.

By continually replaying grievances in their minds, husbands program themselves to be less than loving. By mentally marinating in thoughts of frustration and discontent, wives condition themselves to just go through the motions. It doesn't have to be this way.

In your marriage, do you tend to spend more time dwelling on the past or dreaming together about the future?

You can strengthen your marriage by purposefully becoming your spouse's greatest champion. Anyone can praise, encourage, and build up after the fact, but you can take a proactive role in the quality control of your relationship by affirming the seeds of what is lovely, excellent, and appreciated in your mate . . . before it even shows up. Keep in mind, when you 4:8 your mate, you are also elevating yourself and the whole relationship at the same time. What a deal!

ACTIVATE 4:8

Drill #12

Identify three of your spouse's positive qualities, and to the right of each indicate the significance you find in that trait.

Then, at the bottom, brainstorm a handful of ways you could demonstrate more appreciation for your spouse.

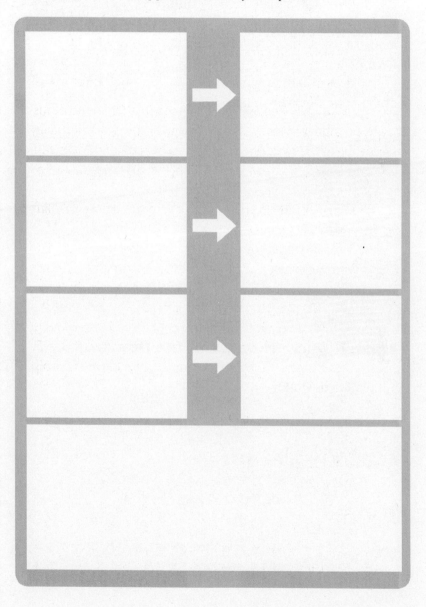

The Extra Mile

Assuming that God intentionally brought you and your mate together, and knowing what you now know as a result of being married, propose four specific reasons why he might have united the two of you. What's the evidence supporting your reasons? Express appreciation to your spouse for the gift of God that he or she represents.

_____

_____

_____

_____

_____

_____

Make It Stick: Thought of the Day

I am my spouse's greatest champion.

Prayer

Heavenly Father, thank you for my spouse and the wonderful plans you have for our relationship. Inspire us both today to align our thoughts, words, and actions with our wedding vows. Amen.

I'LL HAVE WHAT HE'S HAVING

The Joy of Curiosity

IT IS THE GREATEST attitude in the world.

Few if any human assets are as attractive as this particular attitude when it is pure and undiluted. Those possessing it seldom comprehend its incalculable value. When you spot individuals exhibiting this mind-set, you observe that something is quite different about them. Hard to rattle, they are not merely cheerful on the outside; they are peaceful on the inside. Despite their circumstances, they actively appreciate their blessings and remain madly in love with life during good times and bad.

Organically grown, this attitude is established with a decision, nurtured with right thoughts, and time released to the world at large. It will be fiercely tested on the battlefield of life, but fully developed, it cannot be taken away. What is this attitude? I think you already know, don't you?

It is joy.

As we discussed in Day 2, "Deal or No Deal," if you believe that God has great plans for you and your future, it changes things big time. If you truly believe this, you can't hide it from the world. It cannot be contained.

Joy is the irrepressible and contagious fruit of divinely inspired growth. It arises from a deeply entrenched, unshakable belief, the result of sustained right thinking and dwelling on those things that are lovely, admirable, pure, and worthy of praise. Joy is an outward sign of inward faith in God's promises. It is a way of acting, and it is evidence of spiritual maturity.

Scripture is full of references to joy. Psalm 90:14 makes clear that God's love brings us joy: "Satisfy us in the morning with your unfailing love, that we may sing for joy and be glad all our days" (NIV). In addition, joy is a gift from God that comes from trusting him. The apostle Paul writes in Romans 15:13, "May the God of hope fill you with all joy and peace as you trust in him, so that you may overflow with hope by the power of the Holy Spirit" (NIV). Joy is not a distant destination at which you arrive; rather, it's a path you choose to travel each day. The sum and substance of emotional health, joy is an enduring thrill and delight with life, the clear consequence of agreeing with God and behaving in accordance with scriptural truth. It is a state of mind that must be deliberately cultivated if you are determined to live and love and influence others as God intended.

When we witness people having a really good time, our curiosity is activated. We want to know what their secret is, right? We might even want to emulate their approach. If we see someone who has lost a bunch of weight and now looks lean and healthy, we will probably want to know how he did it, especially if we also want to shed a few pounds. If we learn that a neighbor of ours has done extremely well with her invest-ments, we will want to know what her strategy was. When we see a couple of high-character young adults from the same family, we want to know what that mom and dad did that produced such great results. Often at restaurants, we'll pay attention to what the server is bringing to the nearby tables. If we see food that looks delicious, we'll ask the server about it. Haven't you done this before? This curiosity is natural and happens all the time.

For Christians, the main reason that living with joy should be the only way to go is that our example speaks far louder than our words. Our example is either attractive or unattrac-tive. Our example either draws people to the Kingdom or it does not.

When was the last time someone asked you what your secret was? Are you living with joy that looks irresistible to the rest of the world, or are you pretty much living like the rest of the world? Is there anything about your faith that glorifies God more than the joy-filled, super-attractive way that you are leading your life?

Living with joy is our birthright. It is God's intention for all his children. In 1 Thessalonians, the apostle Paul writes, "Rejoice always, pray continually, give thanks in all circum-stances; for this is God's will for you in Christ Jesus" (5:16-18, NIV). As children of God, we are rightful heirs to the blessing of overflowing joy. If we have been reconciled to him through Christ, God has declared us worthy.

As a result, we have a calling and a responsibility to dem-onstrate joy by the way we live. Being joy-filled does not mean that your life is perfect. Who could claim such a distinc-tion? It doesn't even mean that your life is great. What it does mean is that you emphatically trust God and believe that he has great plans for your life, regardless of what is happening right now.

Our human nature, with an assist from modern culture, promotes the idea that solutions must be deep and complicated to be valuable. In most cases, nothing could be further from the truth. Lasting solutions are surprisingly simple. Joy is within us, but it must be released.

Remember, this is your one shot at life. Present the face of joy everywhere you go. Live in such a way that people who watch you will be curious. Live in such a way that they'll conclude, "I'll have what he's having!"

ACTIVATE 4:8

Drill #13

Today's drill forces you to assess the kind of example you've been setting. In the left-hand column on the following page, describe some less-than-joyous recent moments. In the right-hand column, describe a few moments where you clearly shared joy with your world. Then, at the bottom, jot down a few ideas for improving in this area over the next month or so.

The Extra Mile

Do a quick joy audit for the different areas of your life. Rate yourself on a scale of 1 to 5, with 5 being optimal. As a friend, do your words and deeds reflect your faith and the joy of

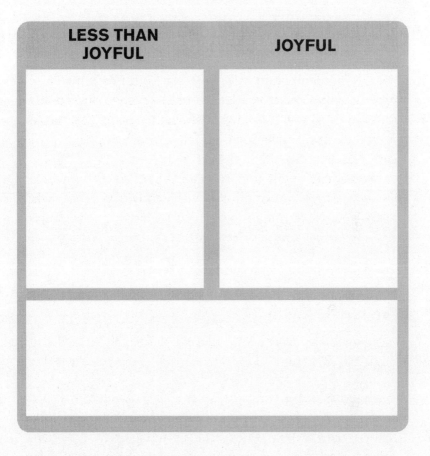

LESS THAN JOYFUL	JOYFUL

your Creator? In your marriage, do your conversations with and about your spouse demonstrate expectation of an awesome future together? As a parent, are your kids likely to live with joy if they model your habits of speech and interaction with others? Do your exercise, nutrition, and sleep routines support a joy-filled life? How about your spiritual life? When was the last time someone, out of curiosity, asked you about your faith?

Make It Stick: Thought of the Day

I am loving life, and it shows!

Prayer

Heavenly Father, thank you for putting joy within my reach. Today, help me to think, speak, and act so that I draw more people to you. Amen.

THE GIFT OF THE PRESENT

The Joy of Right Now

GOD DESIGNED your mind to be immensely powerful. This mental resource is one of the most wonderful blessings from our Creator. Even better, as part of your free will, he gave you command over your mind. This does not mean you must use this power, but it is available.

You can use this dominion over your thought life to maximize your God-given potential, or you can misuse it or even ignore it. The way you think can either multiply your gifts and talents or shrink them. How are you doing in this area? Are you a faithful steward of your mental life?

The Bible clearly teaches that we will reap what we sow. This is so simple, but it can be difficult to put into practice. We sow first, and then we reap. Nowhere is this more apparent than in our thinking. In Galatians 6:7 we are told, "Do not be deceived, God is not mocked; for whatever a man sows, that he will also reap" (NKJV). In 2 Corinthians 9:6, we are warned that if we sow sparingly, we will naturally also reap sparingly, but if we sow bountifully, we will reap bountifully.

Our thoughts, like our actions, have consequences. As relentlessly as you may try, you cannot think one thing and experience something else. You cannot think critically about your spouse, even if you believe it is warranted, and reap true intimacy. You cannot think negatively and live positively any more than you can plant apple seeds and expect to harvest oranges. If you desire to live a joy-filled life—a life that fulfills God's purpose for you—you must keep your thoughts fixed on the things of God.

In your thought life, there's no differentiation between past, present, and future. All you have is right now. This is the gift of the present. A blissful memory is experienced as present joy. A gloomy memory is experienced as present pain. As a result, thinking, talking, and worrying about what you *do not want* can never bring you what you *do want.*

Is it possible to be joy filled without thinking thoughts of joy? Is it possible to worry without thinking worrisome thoughts? Can you be afraid without thinking fearful thoughts? Can you remember a time when you were thinking of hope and happiness but felt depressed at the same time? Can you imagine acting loving while thinking bitter thoughts of anger and resentment? The simple answer is no.

The importance of right thinking is emphasized throughout the Old and New Testaments. In Proverbs, we are taught that "as [a person] thinks in his heart, so is he" (23:7, NKJV) and also that we must "keep [our] heart with all diligence, for out of it spring the issues of life" (4:23, NKJV).

Jesus repeatedly reminds us that what we receive will be the result of what we believe. He underscores this point in the

Sermon on the Mount when he teaches that even to think lust-
ful thoughts is a sin, yet if "your eye is good, your whole body
is filled with light" (Matthew 6:22, NLT). In Matthew 15:18,
we're taught that people are defiled or made unclean not by
what they eat but by what is in their hearts—in other words,
by the way they think.

Jesus knew well that persistent thoughts eventually lead to
action. So did Paul, who encourages us to "take captive every
thought to make it obedient to Christ" (2 Corinthians 10:5,
NIV). Can you imagine a negative, cynical, self-defeating, or
"woe is me" thought being obedient to Jesus Christ?

Finally, in the great simplicity of truth, James sums it up
when he writes that one who doubts is "a double-minded man,
unstable in all his ways" (James 1:8, NKJV). Being duplicitous in
your thinking is the opposite of being mentally disciplined. It's
like praying for sunshine and then grabbing your umbrella as
you walk out the door. It is forgiving your spouse for a grievance and then repeatedly rehashing it in your mind. It is hoping
for the best and secretly fearing the worst. It is the inability to
direct your thoughts in a deliberate, preconceived direction.
Though God's grace doesn't demand mental discipline, living
a life of joyful excellence must be preceded by it.

God has entrusted you with a powerful mind. Use it wisely
to keep your thoughts on the good stuff—and you'll be blessed
with the gift of the present.

ACTIVATE 4:8

Drill #14

What do you think about most of the time? On the following page, identify up to three of your most common thoughts, positive or negative, in the left-hand column. Then in the right-hand column describe the likely effects of those thoughts over time. At the bottom of the page, jot down what changes you are committed to making to improve your thought life.

The Extra Mile

If you can't immediately dissolve negativity, quarantine it. Consider carving out a particular time and place to worry (worry time) and to complain (issue time) each week. As funny as it may sound, this technique helps purify the rest of your week, protecting your emotional health from the minority of negative circumstances that can infect otherwise joyful days. When you cut the spontaneity out of negativity, you severely weaken it. And, when you isolate it, you free up more time to enjoy the gift of the present.

Make It Stick:
Thought of the Day

I appreciate the gift of the present

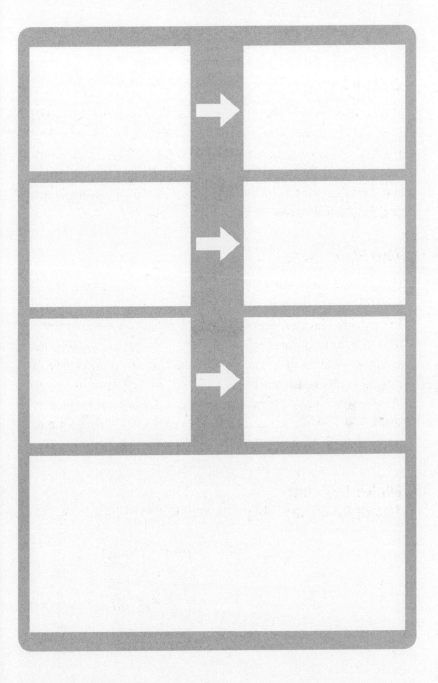

Prayer

God, thank you for the gift of the present moment. Today, protect me from being double minded, and instead, show me how to think in a way that glorifies you and blesses others. Amen.

GRATITUDE SCHMATITUDE

The Profile of an Ingrate

GRATITUDE IS A CONVICTION, a practice, and a discipline.

It's an essential nutrient, a kind of spiritual amino acid for human growth, creativity, and joy. Gratitude involves channeling your energy and attention toward what is present and working rather than toward what's absent and ineffective. And gratitude can be cultivated at ever-deepening levels.

But if gratitude is so vital, why isn't it demonstrated more consistently throughout our culture? In today's lesson, I will outline several common blocks that inhibit an individual's capability to appreciate his or her blessings to the fullest. I've organized these characteristics into what I call "The Profile of an Ingrate." I know it sounds kind of harsh, but after all, how often do you get to use the word *ingrate*? Besides, looking at the subject from this standpoint really drives the message home. In honor of Eeyore, let's continue.

Each of the habits described below can leave us feeling

deficient in gratitude. However, when you are alert to these gratitude blocks, you can minimize their influence so they will not obstruct your potential for joy. Compare yourself with the ingrate profile to identify areas where you could upgrade your gratitude.

Ingrates are disconnected from God. When we are communing daily with our Creator, we experience a spiritual intimacy that almost always melts away grumbling, fear, and other base thoughts that interrupt appreciation of our blessings.

When you are right with God, you humbly cherish life for what it is: a temporary gift, a treasure with an unknown expiration date. This connection with God naturally breeds awe of life, thankfulness for what life has to offer, and gratitude for what you can offer the world with his help. As Jesus said, "I am the vine; you are the branches. If you remain in me and I in you, you will bear much fruit; apart from me you can do nothing" (John 15:5, NIV).

Ingrates are surrounded by excessive noise. By this I am referring to the sheer bombardment of modern life. The constant connection to commitments, obligations, and looming deadlines via virtual offices and smartphones keeps us preoccupied with urgency. Think about it: how often do you receive a call on your mobile phone regarding one of your long-term goals? How often do you receive a text that reminds you to appreciate your spouse or invest more time with your kids? Very rarely. Those tools of convenience are designed to help you react quickly to the immediate demands of the day, not to take action on your most important values.

Ingrates overindulge in the media. Watching excessive television and "over-reading" the newspaper tend to remind us of what's not going well in the world. (On the other hand, doing so provides plenty of material to pray about.) Do you agree that the profusion of media sources seems to provide an avalanche of information but a clear deficit of wisdom? Watching the news exposes us to lots of problems but very few solutions. How much news do we really need? It's a question worth pondering.

This doesn't mean that to be grateful you've got to get rid of your TV or stop reading the newspaper, but you could cut back a little and see if it makes the positive difference for you that it has made for many of my clients. Try it and judge by the results. Often, when you decrease your intake of current events and increase your intake of *positive mental nutrition*, the result is a palpable difference in your outlook.

Ingrates feel entitled. Nothing is quite so powerful, or so quickly destructive to your potential for joy, as the attitude of entitlement. This is the relatively modern notion that someone or some group owes us, that we deserve something from others. With this mind-set, even if we receive something, we don't see it as a gift but as a right. The problem is, those who consume without contributing develop a deep sense of emptiness, which suspends the emotion of gratitude indefinitely.

Moaners and whiners surround us, and they often seem to be competing to see who has the worst grievance against society or who can be the most offended. But entitlement thinking isn't just limited to the national or political stage. Though we may laugh at this dynamic or try to distance ourselves from it, it has seeped into the very fabric of our culture, threatening businesses, families, and future generations.

Closely related to entitlement, but typically on a more interpersonal level, is what I call the Law of Familiarity. This simply means that the longer you've been exposed to a particular blessing, the more likely you are to take it for granted. You begin to feel *entitled* to it rather than being *grateful* for it. To maximize your potential for joy, you must go out of your way to make sure you are not taking for granted the wonderful relationships and other blessings in your life. Remember, gratitude expands joy, and entitlement shrinks it.

Ingrates predict the worst. This kind of negative forecasting is what we typically call worry. When we are concerned and conscientious, we take productive action, but worry involves dwelling on potential negative outcomes *without doing anything about them.* It is the result of dwelling on what you hope won't happen but fear *probably will happen*!

Worry is when you trust your fears more than you trust God. In the two verses immediately preceding Philippians 4:8, Paul writes, "Don't worry about anything; instead, pray about everything. Tell God what you need, and thank him for all he has done. Then you will experience God's peace, which exceeds anything we can understand. His peace will guard your hearts and minds as you live in Christ Jesus" (Philippians 4:6-7, NLT). In these verses we're taught that we need to bypass worry. Instead of taking the passive approach of anxiety, Paul tells us to take the proactive approach of bringing our concerns to God. Once we've done that, we can turn our thoughts to gratitude, thanking God and reminding ourselves of what he has already accomplished in our lives.

The worst part of worry is that it displaces and then dissolves genuine thoughts of gratitude. You cannot worry and be grateful at the same moment. You can waver, of course. You can worry for a few moments, be grateful for a few moments, worry for a few moments, and so on. Ever had a day like this? I know I have. But it doesn't have to be like this. When you deliberately concentrate on current blessings or even future blessings, worry fades away. It drops out of your life.

Of course, this takes a little practice, but you will experience progress the first time you give it a try. It's been helpful for me to remember these words from Mark Twain: "I have been through some terrible things in my life, some of which actually happened." Remember, most of what we worry about never comes to pass.

Ingrates suffer from CDS, which is an abbreviation for my made-up term *Continuous Deficiency Syndrome*. In short, we're always aware that we could have more. This part curse, part blessing comes with the territory of being human and has inspired technological breakthroughs and other societal advances over the centuries. In a sense, our consumer society owes its very existence to its flair for fueling discontentment and an unquenchable appetite for more stuff. We are bombarded with thousands of marketing images every day reminding us that

We could be richer.
Our spouse could be even better.
We could be thinner.
Our breath could be fresher.
Our whites could be whiter.
Our carpets could be cleaner.
Our children could be smarter, more popular, or more
    athletic.

CDS can dominate our attitudes unless we consciously counteract it with gratitude. The more we seek to become satisfied as consumers, the emptier we can become as human beings. That's because ingratitude leaves us in a state of deprivation in which we are constantly pursuing something else. Gratitude, on the other hand, makes us feel that we have enough. Think about it. Where have you been looking for satisfaction recently? Material possessions? Intellectual distinction? Social standing? In light of your past experience, why do you think you will be happy with just a little bit more? Learn to be content with what you have.

Ingrates rush to get the first piece of the pie. This scarcity mentality comes from an all-too-common belief that the pie of abundance contains only a fixed number of pieces. It's the deep-rooted fear that there is not enough of the "good stuff" for everyone. Of course, God's creation is not limited in the least, but when we mistakenly think it is, then for all practical purposes, it is—for us. A scarcity mind-set is characterized by thoughts such as *If she wins, then I lose* or *If he gets those, then I don't.*

But consider that you can bake a bigger pie. You can create more value in your home, in your community, and in the world, and this abundance is self-perpetuating. The more you create, the more people are impacted, and the more abundance is multiplied. You experience lasting abundance only when you realize that you already have everything you need for total joy.

The deficient life of an ingrate is not for you! Look honestly at these barriers to gratitude, consider which ones have a stronghold in your life, and resolve to get rid of them, beginning today. Pursue gratitude relentlessly.

ACTIVATE 4:8 :::::::::::::::::::::::::::::::::

Drill #15

Consider the person you are striving to become. Then, in the left-hand column, identify any habits or characteristics that may be inhibiting your gratitude. In the right-hand column, list some of your gratitude-enhancing habits. At the bottom, write down one positive change you are determined to make in the next week.

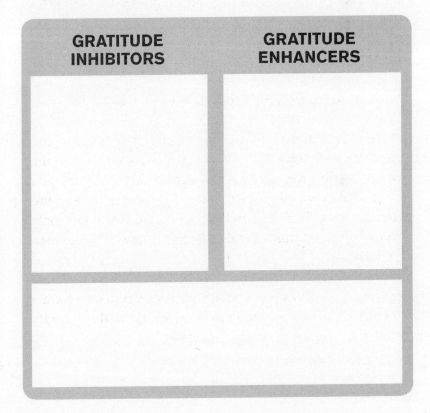

GRATITUDE INHIBITORS	GRATITUDE ENHANCERS

The Extra Mile

To rapidly purge toxic attitudes like ingratitude, take a "4:8 Fast." Purify your thinking one day at a time by abstaining from all complaining, commiserating, fearmongering, criticizing, excuse making, gossiping, and worrying whatsoever! Start with a twenty-four-minute fast and gradually discipline your mind to repel ingratitude and all negativity for a whole day . . . and then a whole week . . . and then. . . . Focus on progress. Rinse and repeat as necessary.

Make It Stick: Thought of the Day

> I organize my lifestyle
> for chronic gratitude.

Prayer

Lord, I am grateful to be connected to you, protected by you, and perfected through you. Help me today to stay sensitive to the goodness and blessings that surround me. Amen.

FEELING VS. FACT

The Joy of the Truth

LATE ONE NIGHT when I was about twelve years old, my family's home burglar alarm went off around midnight. (If you read *The 4:8 Principle,* you may remember this story, but it makes the point so well I have no choice but to use it again.) I was at home with one of my older sisters when the siren began screaming. Startled, we first presumed it was a false alarm—until the system's control panel, via infrared beams positioned in our hallways, indicated that an intruder was moving through the house. Even though we knew the police were on the way, we were terrified.

At one point, we were both hunched down near a side door trying to decide whether to stay in the house or make a run for it. With the siren still going and our hearts racing, I suddenly realized something significant: we had mistakenly set the alarm in "away" mode, which is the setting for when no one will be at home.

I remember standing up not so boldly, silencing the siren, and explaining to my sister what I thought had happened: she had walked down the stairs on the way to the kitchen and had been detected by the interior beam. As I rushed through the house to find her, I, too, was detected. *We* were the "intruders" moving through the house! We had incorrectly programmed the burglar alarm, causing it to go off for no valid reason.

This is easy for us to do with our emotional lives as well. We can inadvertently program ourselves to react a certain way, even if that reaction is not based on reality. We cannot trust our feelings to be synonymous with facts. To paraphrase the humorist Josh Billings, "It's what we know that ain't true that causes us so much trouble."

The single biggest mistake people make when dealing with difficult feelings is accepting them as true. A paradigm shift for many is learning to value what is true and right simply because it is true, not only because it *feels* true. By agreeing with God's truth about ourselves, we can avoid falling into the trap of self-deception, believing those things that we feel like believing, whether or not they have been fact-checked against God's Word.

Feelings are data that you must filter through your reason. Feelings can be deceptive if they are not evaluated in light of the facts and spiritual truth associated with them. Our feelings are one of God's most important built-in feedback devices. But you and your feelings are not one and the same. You are much more than your feelings, and they will not define you unless you allow them to do so.

The longer you have been led by your feelings, the harder it will be to establish reason as the basis for future decision making. Our culture celebrates empathy, enabling, and emotion-driven morality. Succinctly put, I'm told that if it feels right in my heart, then I should do it. Yet it is through our feelings that we are most typically led astray.

Consider the ten decisions from your past that you most regret. How many of these choices were based on reasoned evaluation of facts, in light of God's principles and purpose for your life? Most adults can look back on their life experiences and recall very poor decisions that felt right at the time, as well as very smart decisions that felt not so right at the time. Even now, most of us have blind spots that keep us stubbornly chained to our feelings, irrationally neglecting to do those things that would make our lives and relationships stronger.

We must remember that emotions are only subjective indicators of objective experience. For example, if you are hiking through the woods and you come across what you believe to be a snake in the path ahead of you, you will respond emotionally to that belief. You may experience fear and stop in your tracks or quickly retreat. Whatever your response, it's rooted in how you interpret what you're observing with your senses.

Imagine that as you step back, you look a little more closely and realize that the "snake" is in fact only a rope lying in the path. You interpreted it as a snake, and then your emotions, followed by your body, reacted to what you *thought* you saw. It didn't matter that the rope lying in the path was no threat at all. Perception was reality. You believed it to be true.

It is easy to do this in all sorts of situations, especially with the important people in your life. For example, it is quite common for spouses to express irritation with the exact qualities in their mate that seemed so attractive while they were dating. Sometimes it takes a very good and diplomatic friend to point out that the reality has not changed—only the perception. Have you ever experienced this?

Remember, *when your interpretations change, your emotions change.* That means you are not a victim of your emotions; you can shape them by the way you choose to think. Your job is to keep the emotional spiral pointing upward. Your task is to become proficient at interpreting the events of your life in such a way that you remain empowered to improve them. If your teenager loses her cool, keep yours by assuming she's dealing with something difficult and unrelated to you. In this way, you retain the poise to help her improve the situation. We'll discuss many more options for neutralizing negative emotions throughout the remainder of the book.

How about you? Are you chasing the truth or following the feeling?

ACTIVATE 4:8 ::::::::::::::::::::::::::::::

Drill #16

In what circumstances have you historically felt most rattled or threatened? On the following page, indicate up to four fear thoughts in the left-hand column. To the right, identify God's truth that addresses that type of thinking.

The Extra Mile

As if completing a personal journal entry, recall one poor decision and one smart decision that you have made in either the

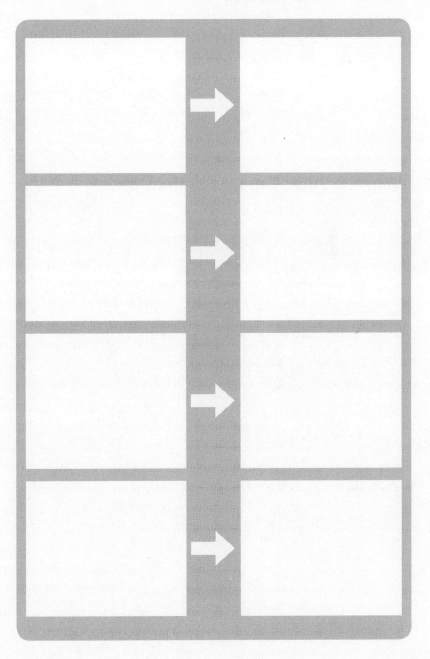

distant or recent past. Reflect on both, writing down how you felt prior to each decision and noting how your feelings likely influenced your decisions. Then consider this: if a loved one were faced with a similar decision and came to you for advice, how would you counsel him or her? How are your feelings swaying your decisions from day to day?

Make It Stick: Thought of the Day

I filter my feelings through God's promises.

Prayer

Jesus, thank you that I am not my feelings. Today, teach me to agree with you and value what is true and right simply because it is true, not only because it happens to feel true. Amen.

HUNTING RATS

The Joy of Being Battle Ready

IMAGINE A POT of water boiling on the stove. If you dump a bunch of ice in the boiling water, it will stop boiling—but only temporarily, because the source of heat has not been addressed.

Now imagine that the boiling water is your negative emotions and the source of heat is erroneous thought patterns that have become automatic over time. To stop negativity and upgrade your potential for joy, you must either have lots of "ice" or you must correct the negative thinking. The ice may take different forms: excessive food, television, or alcohol; drugs; chronic busyness; or physical escapes. All these chill the water momentarily but do nothing to eliminate the cause of the heat. Even when you vent or "let off steam" by removing the pot's lid, you are only temporarily keeping the water from boiling over and making a mess. The only way to stop the water permanently is to look underneath the pot and adjust the source.

We do all sorts of silly things that fuel our negative emotions.

As a result, we end up getting more of *what we don't want*. We distort things, we exaggerate things, we amplify our experiences in life, and then we pick the wrong things to dwell on. Philippians 4:8 clearly communicates *what we should do:* Dwell on the things that are uplifting. Dwell on the things that are working. Dwell on the things that are worthy of praise. In other words, dwell on the good stuff.

When you find yourself emotionally low, you can be pretty sure that you've been dwelling on the not-so-good stuff. In this low state, your mind plays tricks on you. If you're trying to implement the 4:8 Principle, it is important to start noticing your emotions and how they spiral quickly upward or downward. This increased awareness shifts you from being the passenger in your emotional life to being the driver. Only when you notice changes in your emotional life can you begin to rise above the passive choices that fuel negative emotions.

Some negative thoughts stand out more than others. These "Really Awful Thoughts," or what I call RATs for short, terrorize your potential for joy. In today's lesson, I will teach you how to spot them so that you can have a counterattack plan ready. After identifying the most common RATs, I will show you how to disrupt, dispute, and then deflect them. Keep in mind that these RATs highlight crooked *thinking patterns,* not crooked people. See if you can relate to any of the patterns described below.

Amplifiers magnify unpleasant situations with recurrent use of extreme words like *always, never, no one,* and *every time.* The truth is, virtually nothing in life falls in that excessive category. These amplifiers frequently show up in marriage and parenting. Aside from being distortions, these statements cause everyone involved to plummet below the joy zone.

Feelers accept negative feelings as true without questioning them. Sometimes your negative emotions reveal a deficiency in yourself or someone else, and sometimes they don't. Often what you feel is a simple distortion. It may reflect the quality of your thinking more than it does the quality of your life experience. While feelings are important, they are no substitute for the truth.

Guessers pretend they know what other people are thinking, and then they assume the worst. This often triggers an emotional response from the other person, which in turn gets you defensive. This kicks off a cycle that is not very joyful.

Exaggerators transform molehills into mountains with trigger words like *horrible, worst, ruined, shocked, devastated, stunned,* and *outraged.* I like to think of this as "awfulizing" or "drama queen syndrome."

Identifiers inject harmless events with personal meaning. They take things too personally and interpret negative events as personal attacks. For example, if I get cut off in traffic and spill coffee in my lap, I might respond as if the other driver had been out to get me. Momentarily, I act as if I believe the other driver had carefully plotted to be at just that spot on the interstate, at just the right angle to cut me off. Once he identified my car, he thought, *Ah, that's Tommy. Got him,* and then drove right in front of me on purpose.

Forecasters predict the worst-case scenario, usually aloud, before they even get started.

Cynics have a knack for finding something wrong, even if it is the *only* thing wrong. Despite the good, they use their mental radar to see the bad. Because there's always going to be some degree of bad stuff, cynics will forever be able to justify their viewpoint. Know anyone like this? Their reward is that they get to be more miserable.

Blamers point the finger at someone else for their own problems, even though it's rare that problems are caused entirely by someone else. As the opposite of responsibility, blame is so popular because it temporarily liberates you. It gives you a short-term emotional fix; you feel better for the time being. However, blaming others is ultimately immobilizing. It holds you back and cuts the legs right out from under your full potential for joy. Blame is like an emotional dirty bomb.

Justifiers remind themselves of all the reasons why they are entitled to this negative emotion or that negative outburst. Losing sight of their vision, justifiers are advocates for their own negativity. It manifests in language like "If you only knew what he did" or "I deserve to be upset."

Not exactly the stuff that joy is made of, is it? Now that you are aware of these RATs, in tomorrow's lesson I'll show you how to exterminate them and put an end to the games they orchestrate in your mind.

ACTIVATE 4:8 :::::::::::::::::::::::::::::::

Drill #17

What Really Awful Thoughts (RATs) bug you the most? On the following page, identify up to three of your most common RATs, and to the right, indicate under what circumstances those RATs seem to thrive. At the bottom, jot down a few ideas for counteracting those thoughts.

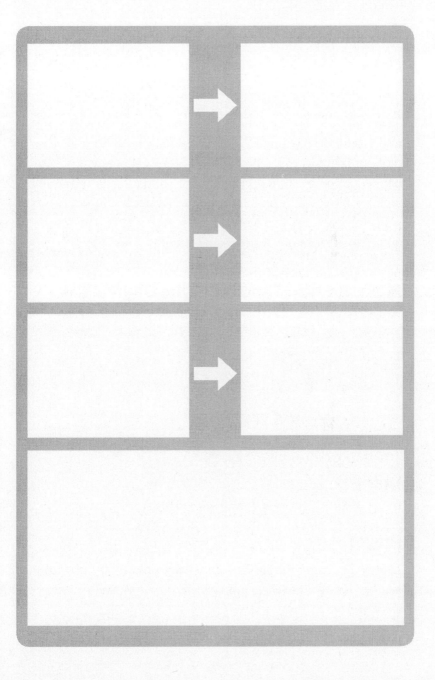

The Extra Mile

Develop a ritual for surrendering your subconscious mind to God right before going to sleep each night. Simply confess any unhealthy thought patterns, especially RATs that you are aware of, and then ask God to replace them with thoughts that would be pleasing to him. Plead with him to purify your thought life at its roots. As you drift off to sleep, practice dropping your assumptions and conclusions and refilling your mind with God's wisdom and creativity. Give it a try in your own way. Remember, while we may sleep each night, God doesn't, and neither does our subconscious mind.

Make It Stick: Thought of the Day

My thinking creates upward emotional spirals!

Prayer

Lord, thank you for freeing me from entrenched negativity. Today, help me to avoid emotional breakdowns and instead experience emotional breakthroughs. Amen.

DAY
18

ACKNOWLEDGE AND CHALLENGE

The Joy of Emotional Strength

IN HARMONY with cause and effect, our feelings change after our focus changes. Our emotions function as a kind of self-service feedback mechanism that helps us evaluate the quality of our thought lives—and make corrections as necessary. In essence, our emotions allow us to feel what we've been thinking about. If we feel terrific about life, that's a reliable indicator that our most recent thinking has been healthy and constructive.

However, feeling that our lives are wonderful certainly does not mean that our lives are 100 percent wonderful; rather, it means that we are focusing on those components of our lives that seem to be going really well at the moment, while simultaneously downplaying our existing dissatisfactions. This dynamic is why we consider life to be "wonderful" right now. But with a few negative prompts here and there (and especially if we harbor some "Really Awful Thoughts" or RATs), we can lose this 4:8 Perspective, start focusing on frustrations, and quickly feel rotten rather than wonderful.

Consider that many individuals living in modest conditions express great joy for life. On the flip side, many people who seem to be highly blessed demonstrate great discontent with their circumstances. Clearly, our emotional lives are not always indicative of the external quality of our lives. Our emotions are most certainly not objective indicators of how our lives are progressing.

To make wise decisions, let your goals and your reason—not your emotions—guide you. To live a life of maximum joy, learn the methods for minimizing negative emotions so they will not dominate your life.

When we deal with negative emotions, we have a couple of straightforward choices: we can *suppress* them by keeping them buried inside, ultimately making ourselves sick. Or we can *express* our negativity to those closest to us (closest either in proximity or in relationship) and make *them* "sick" in the short term. For many people, suppression and expression are the only tools in their emotional toolbox. As the old proverb goes, "If the only tool you have is a hammer, then everything starts to look like a nail." But it doesn't have to be this way. There are other ways to effectively manage negative emotions. Let me explain.

Imagine covering a small campfire with a bucketful of dirt. What happens? Instantly the fire is snuffed out. Now think about the mental process you followed prior to smothering it. First you developed the desire to put out the fire, probably because you were leaving the campground or going to sleep. Then you made the decision to do so. Finally you took action—in a way that helped you meet your goal. If your goal was to put out the fire, you would never think of throwing on another log or dousing it with gasoline. You probably wouldn't ignore the fire either, pretending (and falsely hoping) it would eventually burn out by itself during the night. If you gambled on this course of inaction, you might end up with a fire too aggressive to contain.

Negative emotions function in some ways like the campfire. How do you "put them out"? You extinguish them with positive, constructive thinking. You don't ignore them, and you refuse to nourish them with the kind of attention that causes them to erupt into a blazing inferno. Alternatively, you can get out the gas can, dump it on your thought life, and aggravate the situation with inflammatory mental habits, emotional outbursts, and unwise decisions. But why in the world would you want to do that? If you have the desire to triumph over negative emotions, and you have made the decision to do so, here are two field-tested approaches that will help you immensely.

First, *acknowledge your negative emotions.* God doesn't want you to be in constant emotional pain any more than he wants you to be in constant physical pain. Your ideal state, both physically and emotionally, is one of health, harmony, and balance.

Physical pain indicates that an injury or imbalance needs to be addressed. Typically, when we experience pain, we acknowledge these bodily signals and take action to correct them. You would never think of continuing to sprint around the track if your knee was swollen with fluid. However, on the emotional side, we often ignore similar signs and continue thinking and behaving as before. It is helpful to think of a negative emotion as a warning light on your car's dashboard. If you ignore the indicator light, you may very well be inviting a bigger problem down the road. If you don't deal with it, the warning remains front and center wherever you go.

Once you acknowledge the problem by taking your car in to get checked out, you can discover whether it's a real problem or a false alarm. Any necessary maintenance can be performed, and the caution light will disappear. In the same way, you can defuse your negative emotions by acknowledging their presence. Determine whether any critical needs are going unmet. Are you frightened or threatened in some way? Are you tired? Hungry? Feeling unloved or disrespected? Just as we are most vulnerable to sickness when our immune system is compromised by lack of sleep or poor nutrition, we are most vulnerable to negativity when our emotional health is compromised by unmet needs. Negative emotions tend to surface most intensely when accompanied by an unmet need. If there's a need you can address, take care of it. If it's a false alarm, acknowledge the feelings and move on.

Second, *challenge the legitimacy of your negative emotions.* When you become aware of a negative emotion, simply remind yourself, "This is just the way I feel. It's not necessarily the truth. It doesn't need to dictate my behavior." Feelings are not the gospel and are seldom cited in Scripture as a basis for taking action. They should not be ignored, but neither should they be worshiped.

Left unchecked, your feelings tend to drag you into the worst aspects of human nature—namely, shifting your attention and outlook from the long term to the short term. Instead of allowing your feelings to guide your decisions, allow God's Word to be your compass. Compliance with God's principles is the seldom discussed, timeless secret to sustained positive emotions.

If you are held captive to how the world wants you to feel and behave, you must also endure the roller coaster of negative emotions that corresponds with that philosophy. Don't be a pushover for negative emotions. Make a commitment today to challenge the validity of cloudy emotions. Put them in their place so that you realize they are not the basis for your decisions.

ACTIVATE 4:8

Drill #18

Simply being aware of your negative patterns helps diminish them. On the following page, identify three of your most common negative emotions and, to the right, the trigger or catalyst for each emotion. At the bottom, write down one thing you are going to do differently to stay positive and composed.

The Extra Mile

Write a letter to yourself acknowledging two or three recurring negative emotions (if you have any) and what you believe to be the primary cause of the negativity. Rambling is encouraged in this exercise. Once you've identified the reasons for the poor feelings, examine them and challenge their authenticity. (Warning: If you succeed in justifying your negative emotions, you get to keep them.) Conclude your letter with a clearly worded resolution to live with joy no matter what.

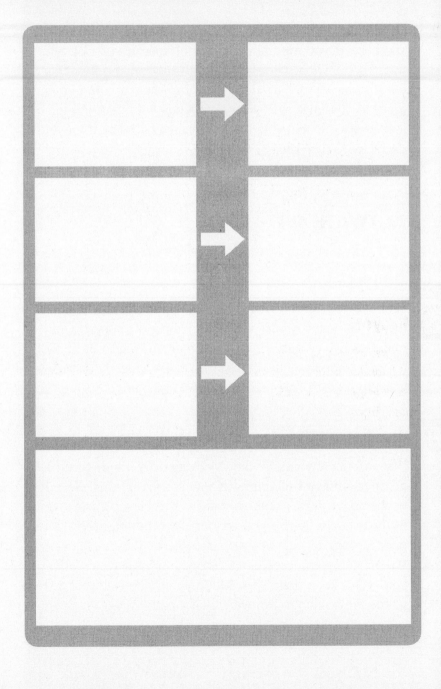

Make It Stick: Thought of the Day

> God rules my life, not my emotions!

Prayer

Father, thank you for inventing both positive and negative emotions and for the feedback each one provides. Help me today to make decisions in compliance with your principles, no matter how I happen to feel. Amen.

JUST EXCHANGE IT

The Joy of an Easy Return Policy

OUR MIND'S POLICY is clear cut.

You cannot eliminate a thought directly; only exchanges are permitted. Resisting an unwanted thought only entangles you and drives that thought deeper into your mind, making it even more of a distraction. Attempting to get rid of an unproductive thought by fighting it or trying to block it out will not work. You can do away with a negative thought only when you exchange it with a positive thought. I call this the Law of Exchange.

If you like, you can also purge positive thoughts by substituting negative thoughts. I don't know why anyone would want to, but that option, as you've probably observed, seems to be widely practiced.

Your conscious mind is never inactive. While you are awake, it engages in some level of thought, either helpful or hurtful. If you do not deliberately plant and nurture the right thoughts, the wrong ones will take over like weeds in a deserted garden. Your conscious mind also holds only one thought at a time, and that single thought is either in alignment with your potential for joy or it is not. This is good news because it means you can swap an average thought with a brilliant thought or a fearful thought with a courageous thought whenever you choose.

If you are upset with your spouse and tell yourself not to be upset, you stay tuned in to what is aggravating you, and your mood may even worsen. If we're playing golf and I say to you, "Don't think about hitting your ball into the trap," of course you immediately think of doing so. If you say, "I will not hit my ball into the trap," you're still thinking about it. Your brain finds it very difficult to concentrate on the reverse of something.

The solution is to transfer your attention to something else completely. When you switch to a higher channel mentally, you replace the previous, lower channel. You can exert far greater control over your thinking and, by extension, your life by exchanging negative, counterproductive thoughts for positive, empowering thoughts.

Thoughts of sand traps and hazards are displaced with precise thoughts about where you want your ball to land on the green. Thoughts of discontent with your spouse are replaced with thoughts of appreciation for the overall relationship or advance gratitude for the great future God surely has planned for both of you. Thoughts of boldness replace thoughts of doubt. Thoughts of winning dislodge thoughts of losing. You overcome evil with good.

And when you preoccupy your mind with God's Word, you go a long way toward shutting out temptation. By committing Scripture verses to memory, you begin the process of forcing out negative, limiting thoughts and replacing them with the marvelous power and potential of God's promises. Remember, the Word of God does not lie dormant once internalized:

The word of God is alive and powerful. It is sharper than the sharpest two-edged sword, cutting between soul and spirit, between joint and marrow. It exposes our innermost thoughts and desires. (Hebrews 4:12, NLT)

In addition to Philippians 4:8, you will find the verses below to be especially worthy of memorization. As you explore the Bible, you will find an unlimited supply of these spiritual gems, all of which are especially useful in elevating your state of mind. When you store these inspirational truths in your memory bank, you will be thrilled with the joy and strength you receive.

- "God is our refuge and strength, an ever-present help in trouble" (Psalm 46:1, NIV).
- "You guide me with your counsel, leading me to a glorious destiny" (Psalm 73:24, NLT).
- "Trust in the LORD with all your heart and lean not on your own understanding; in all your ways submit to him, and he will make your paths straight" (Proverbs 3:5-6, NIV).
- "You will keep in perfect peace all who trust in you, all whose thoughts are fixed on you!" (Isaiah 26:3, NLT).
- "Jesus said, 'Come to me, all of you who are weary and carry heavy burdens, and I will give you rest'" (Matthew 11:28, NLT).
- "The Kingdom of God is already among you" (Luke 17:21, NLT).
- "You will know the truth, and the truth will set you free" (John 8:32, NLT).

- "The thief comes only to steal and kill and destroy; I have come that they may have life, and have it to the full" (John 10:10, NIV).
- "I am leaving you with a gift—peace of mind and heart. And the peace I give is a gift the world cannot give. So don't be troubled or afraid" (John 14:27, NLT).
- "Forgetting the past and looking forward to what lies ahead, I press on to reach the end of the race and receive the heavenly prize for which God, through Christ Jesus, is calling us" (Philippians 3:13-14, NLT).
- "I can do everything through Christ, who gives me strength" (Philippians 4:13, NLT).
- "God has not given us a spirit of fear and timidity, but of power, love, and self-discipline" (2 Timothy 1:7, NLT).

There is no need to cling to thoughts that haven't produced joyful fruit in your life. If you want to gain emotional control, first gain mental control. Build a better attitude of mind, one thought at a time. You hold the power. If you try on a new thought and it doesn't work for you, exchange it.

ACTIVATE 4:8

Drill #19

Nothing pushes out toxic thoughts like God thoughts! On the following page, identify three Bible verses that you'd like to commit to memory. Then memorize them, of course! I recommend that you write one verse each week on a 3 x 5 card and carry it with you for the entire week, rereading it ten or twenty times a day.

The Extra Mile

Become hypersensitive to your thought life. Since you can be negative only when you're thinking 8:4 Thoughts, you can quickly become positive by thinking 4:8 Thoughts. The split second you notice an unproductive thought running through your mind, replace it with something like, "I am responsible," "I trust God," "God is with me," "This is temporary," or "I can do it with God's help." Repeat, repeat, repeat! Be ready with your comeback before the heat of the moment. Make negative, limiting thoughts unwelcome in your mind.

 ## Make It Stick: Thought of the Day

I think productive thoughts all day long!

Prayer

Heavenly Father, thank you for designing my mind to hold but one thought at a time. Help me today to purposely preoccupy my mind with your Word, which is the greatest of all thoughts. Amen.

VISUALIZE GOD'S BLESSINGS!

The Joy of Imagination

YOU AND I VISUALIZE daily. Surprised? *Visualization* is simply a term that means "imagining the future." Each of us engages in this mental process numerous times throughout the day.

Ambitious young baseball players visualize playing in the big leagues. Restless teenagers happily imagine graduation day and what college life might be like. Many young women clearly visualize the details of their wedding day long before it happens. Newly married couples frequently envision their future children playing in the backyard. Business leaders mentally rehearse important presentations well ahead of delivering them to clients. Successful entrepreneurs visualize new customers and the rewards that correspond with increasing their service in the marketplace.

In today's lesson, though, I am encouraging you to become intentional with your imagination. The alternative is to allow random images, triggered from your past experiences and current mood, to occupy your mind, but as you know by now, that is not a very 4:8 thing to do.

God designed you and me with the mental capability to envision a better future, to imagine things as they *could be* rather than just as they are. This is most obvious when we pray. We are always led to pray for something better, not for something worse. In effect, as human beings, God has given us the power to experience what we visualize, but most people visualize only what already exists. As the only part of his creation with this capacity, we should be quite grateful.

This concept is so simple yet profound that it is worth repeating: *We have been given the power to experience what we visualize, but we tend to visualize only that which we already experience.* As long as you fix your mind only on what you have today, you will very likely receive nothing different tomorrow. If you persistently hold mental pictures of the past and present, it's unlikely that you will travel far from those images in reality.

We all have the capability to envision a wonderful future or an improved condition in our lives. Unfortunately, many people spend far more time visualizing what they don't want than what they do want. Then they insecurely make decisions based on the fear and worry these mental images generate.

Unquestionably, a clear vision for the future is a precondition to reaching your full potential here on earth. Without such vision, individuals, couples, families, organizations, and entire civilizations drift and meander, squandering opportunities for positive influence that can spring only from having a clearly envisioned path for the future. This power to visualize can be used or discarded; it is your decision. But choosing to pass along this opportunity also means passing on some of the life-enhancing joy that God has planned for you and for all of his children.

Visualization is used by successful people in all fields, especially in athletics, entertainment, and more recently in medicine to support the healing process in patients. As part of God's perfect design, visualization works because it relies on the human brain's tendency to fulfill its most dominant thought. Because the subconscious mind cannot distinguish between a real event and one that is vividly imagined, when it receives a picture of a goal as if it were already achieved, it interprets this as a fact and responds accordingly, helping to remove the mental blocks inhibiting attainment.

In light of this understanding, the most effective way to expand your potential is to constantly expose your mind to a multisensory image of the *end result* you're striving for. This image serves as a command to the brain to reproduce outwardly what was created inwardly.

I encourage you not to approach the visualization process randomly or haphazardly. If you are willing to train your mind, you will be much better prepared to carry out the work God has called you to do. Your responsibility is to deliberately feed your mind crisp, vivid pictures of the person God wants you to become. This starts with practicing the 4:8 Principle. Certainly, God's vision for your future is lovely, excellent, and worthy of praise—even well beyond your ability to imagine it!

To get started, set aside four or five minutes every day to visualize yourself, in as much detail as possible, living a joy-filled life. See yourself fully alive, loving your work and having a strong, positive impact. Envision yourself completely engaged and energized at home with your family. Rehearse these ideal scenarios frequently with as much clarity as possible.

The two best times to practice visualization are right before you go to sleep and just after waking in the morning. Consider incorporating this into your Fifteen-Minute Miracle. Get relaxed and calm with the help of a few deep breaths. Then step into your own mental movie. See yourself doing what you would be doing if your prayer had been answered or your goal had already been accomplished. If you persist in holding the image of the life you believe God wants for you, that image is much more likely to become a fact.

ACTIVATE 4:8

Drill #20

Imagine using your talents to accomplish something really important to you. Envision what that would look like. On the following page, first write what you would see happening if your goal were already a reality. Then identify who would be blessed as a result of your efforts. Be exhaustive here. Finally, reread your first two answers and then describe all the emotions you will experience when you achieve this special goal.

The Extra Mile

The next time you pray about a particular problem, challenge, or issue currently facing you, take a few extra minutes to get relaxed before you begin. Take six or seven slow, deep breaths while imagining that your mind is completely free of old opinions, preconceived notions, your own knowledge, or entrenched negativity of any kind. Then ask God to fill your empty mind with his perfect wisdom. Affirm that you are open

and receptive to direct inspiration from God—and mean it. Then visualize Jesus sitting next to you, coaching and advising you. Dwell upon the love, peace, and understanding in his eyes as you gladly receive his guidance. Finally, thank God for his perfect solution. Experience the surge of confidence you would have following such an encounter. This opportunity is ready when you are.

Make It Stick: Thought of the Day

I envision what I
intend to experience!

Prayer

Lord, I am grateful that you have granted me the power to imagine life as it could be rather than just as it is right now. Coach me today to use this capability to move closer to, not further from, the person you created me to become. Amen.

A CRY FOR HELP

The Joy of Compassion

NOW THAT WE'RE HALFWAY through our forty-day journey, it's time to evaluate. How are you doing so far? Are you making the progress toward abundant joy that you'd like to be making? Do you have a greater sense of confidence in your ability to thwart or at least manage the negativity in this world? Be encouraged by the improvements you see already, and keep your eyes on your goals as you continue to progress.

So far in this book, we've talked about ways we can change our own thoughts and attitudes. But that only goes so far since we're not living in a vacuum. We interact with other people every day, and they can be rewarding or challenging, inspiring or infuriating. How do we respond? In dealing with other people, the chief strategy for staying joyful is to become fluently compassionate, by which I mean that compassion becomes your reflex. What might this look like? When interacting with a difficult person, you automatically think compassionate thoughts. You speak compassionate words. And you engage in compassionate deeds, whether or not you happen to feel like it or believe it to be justified.

You choose compassion because it is a biblically sound virtue that consequently produces biblically sanctioned fruit. When we're compassionate, we're emulating God. Psalm 103:13 says, "As a father has compassion on his children, so the LORD has compassion on those who fear him" (NIV). Also, the apostle Paul encourages us as believers to clothe ourselves with many virtues, one of which is compassion. So when we respond to someone else with compassion, we know we're following God's directions for life.

There is really nothing to lose when taking this approach, but there is much to gain. Of course, this "peace and deference" policy does not come naturally to most people (myself included). That is why today's lesson is essential in our quest for the joy-filled life.

Here's the basis of "fluent compassion": instead of suppressing or expressing negative emotions, you can extend compassion toward the person who seems to be the source of the negativity in the first place—even if it's you. *Assume that problem people are struggling or in pain of some unknown origin.* Accurate or not, this learned belief will help you respond more positively and will also boost your mental and emotional health. If the problem people weren't stressed, they wouldn't be acting so negatively, right? So graciously give them the benefit of the doubt. Adopting this unusual perspective has helped my clients and me tremendously. Is this interpretation of the situation always true? Probably not, but what harm does it cause? Instead of asking, "Does she deserve my compassion?" assume that she does and respond accordingly.

Often we overscrutinize a situation, asking 8:4 Questions, apparently in search of a justification to return negativity with negativity. It doesn't have to be this way. Here are some much better questions to ask when you find yourself pulled toward negative thinking: Is this a useful belief? Is this a belief that will help me experience more joy? Will it cause me to be more empathetic? Will it help me get along better with others? Will it be constructive in my marriage or other relationships?

Earlier in this book, I mentioned that I cut in front of another driver at a four-way stop. Do you remember the other driver's reaction to my mistake? No doubt his rabid behavior was excessive and immature. But it certainly signaled to me that some preexisting trouble existed in his life and because of this, he was worthy of my compassion. It's not like I wanted to invite him over for Sunday dinner or even give him my business card. But I said a quick prayer, refrained from judging him, and never gave it another thought until I began writing this book.

What if I later found out that the obnoxious driver had just received some bad financial news or had been notified that his home was up for foreclosure? What if he had been up all night at the hospital taking care of his son who was near death? Would that change my perspective? Totally! Could we assume similar scenarios every time we encounter a rude driver or difficult person? Yes, if we make the decision outside the heat of the moment to do so.

The real lesson for me that day was that my compassion preserved my joy. I do not suppose that my compassion mattered to the other driver in the slightest, but maybe he cooled down a little more quickly because I did not return fire.

When people respond negatively, attribute it to something

they are dealing with that you don't know about. They are likely just having a tough day. Maybe they are dealing with a heavy burden. Perhaps they just got dumped on by someone else, or maybe they got only two hours of sleep the night before. It is helpful to remember that when someone treats you harshly, it says much more about him or her than about you. But how you respond reveals your character.

Here are three ways to increase your capacity for compassion:

First, *get curious about people.* Being curious about the other person's story activates the Law of Exchange—replacing a negative thought with a positive one. It also causes you to disconnect yourself from the situation and not take it so personally, creating a mental environment far more favorable to compassion.

Second, *remember that most negative outbursts are conditioned responses and not as ominous as they may initially appear.* Other people are living out scripts that were placed in their heads long before you ever met them. You may have acted as the trigger for their response, but you are not the source. Challenge yourself to become the type of individual who is not rattled by the reactions of others.

Third, *realize that most stress and tension are just growth trying to take place.* In fact, wherever there is an absence of productive friction, you are likely to find stagnation—and stagnation does not produce joy. Like our physical muscles, our emotional muscles must be stretched beyond previous limits to become stronger and more resilient. So when you encounter a difficult person, view it as an opportunity for growth.

The only downside to practicing compassion is that at the end of your life you may find out that your positive assumptions about other people weren't perfectly true. Even so, I propose that this is worth doing. Those years will still be better lived than if you had assumed the worst about others. Do you agree? Since we learn our beliefs anyway, why not master this really beneficial one? Remember, when your interpretations change, so do your emotions.

ACTIVATE 4:8

Drill #21

Consider a few of the important relationships in your life. Then, on the following page, identify up to four of these individuals. To the right, note one way that you could extend more compassion to each person.

The Extra Mile

Pick one person to concentrate almost all your 4:8 energy on, just for today. This could be your spouse, child, sibling, friend, parent, business partner, boss, top client, or someone else who is special in your life. Maybe this individual needs your attention because he is facing challenging circumstances, or perhaps you decide to focus on this person simply because she is so important to you. Before you go any further, ask God for guidance in selecting your "target." Don't tell the other person what you are doing, but ask God to use you this day as an ambassador of joy in his or her life.

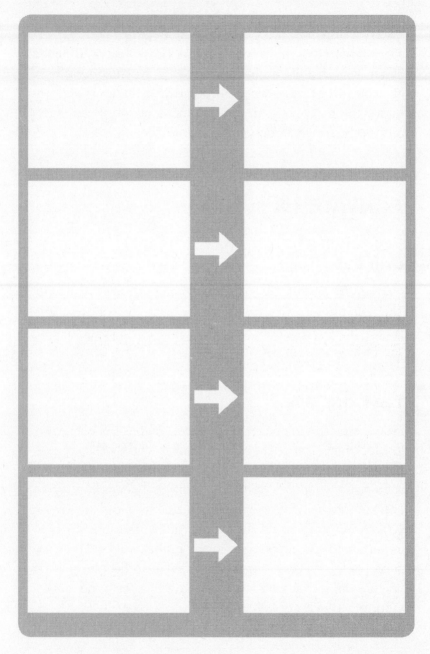

Make It Stick: Thought of the Day

My compassion
protects
my joy!

Prayer

Heavenly Father, thanks for covering me with your grace and mercy. Inspire me today to show compassion for others as you have shown compassion for me. Amen.

WE ARE SPONGES

The Joy of Our Surroundings

WE SOAK UP our environment.

We breathe. We live. We think. We walk. We talk. We work. We pray. We play. And as we do, we absorb the influences of our environment along the way. What we let into our hearts sways our beliefs, feelings, values, expectations, and actions. Nothing comes out of our hearts except that which we put there first. In Proverbs 4:23, the wisest man who ever lived put it like this: "Above all else, guard your heart, for everything you do flows from it" (NIV).

To a greater degree than is probably comfortable for us to acknowledge, we are where we are at this point in our lives because of the dominating thoughts that we have allowed to occupy our minds and hearts. Your emotional and physical health, your marriage and family life, your career and personal economy, as well as your connection with God have been, and continue to be, heavily influenced by the quality of your mental diet. The soundest way to improve the quality of your life is to first improve the quality of your thinking. And the best way to improve the quality of your thinking is to keep vigilant watch over your heart.

Many people downplay the power of the human mind because it is easier to attribute their chronic dissatisfaction to something other than themselves than it is to own their life situations entirely. Claiming responsibility for the conditions of your life is difficult—sometimes dreadfully difficult. However, doing so marks the beginning of an upward spiral toward greater joy, greater satisfaction, and greater freedom from negative emotions. Early and often, I tell my clients that the highest form of individual responsibility is responsibility for their thought lives. All mental work is delayed and all upward progress is deferred until this is acknowledged.

When you guard your heart, you are preserving your joy. When you guard your heart, you are calculating the potential cost of what enters your mind, either to visit temporarily or to reside permanently. When you guard your heart, you are protecting your mental software from negative scripts, bad code, and harmful viruses. To guard your heart is to shield your mind from the environmental hazards that can steer your thinking away from what is true, pure, lovely, and excellent. When we filter out 8:4 stimuli that are joy reducing, we are, by extension, only granting access to 4:8 stimuli that are joy producing. Think about it: We protect our president. We protect our families. We protect our businesses. We protect our homes. We protect our cars. It's critical that we protect our minds. This is a big job.

I have observed that even well-meaning Christian men and women pay very little attention to their frequent exposures. They listen to whatever happens to be playing on the radio. They watch the trendy television programs everyone else is watching. They read the popular books everyone else is reading. Like almost everyone else, they ingest whatever news headlines pop in front of their eyes. They participate agreeably in the random conversations of the day, all with very little intention or premeditation. Unsurprisingly, like most everyone else, they experience a palpable shortfall of joy in their relationships and in their lives as a whole.

Far too many followers of Christ follow the culture instead of wisely guarding their hearts and feeding their minds. They take a very casual and impulsive approach to what they read, watch, and listen to on an ongoing basis. Their mental diet differs little, if at all, from their secular counterparts. And since they, like all of us, soak up their surroundings, they ever so gradually absorb the culture's fashionable worldview and corresponding value system.

Your mental diet impacts your character and, as a result, directly or indirectly influences every decision you make. To maximize your joy and live an exceptional life, you must become picky about your daily inputs. You cannot grant yourself an "All-Access Pass" to popular culture and still maintain joy at the highest levels. While there is no way to avoid these cultural weeds entirely, you can minimize the damage by being highly selective in what you choose to expose yourself to on a regular basis.

As you evaluate what you are feeding your mind, consider these questions:

1. In what ways am I growing as a result of the books I am reading?
2. What captures my attention before falling asleep at night and upon awakening in the morning?
3. How is my use of social media helping me meet my goals?

4. How do the movies and TV shows I watch affect my attitudes toward faith, family, and work?
5. How could I better use my drive time to grow, learn, and stay inspired?
6. What biographies and autobiographies have I read or listened to in the last twelve months?
7. Does my home library show I am a serious student of life? How so?
8. What are my reading, listening, and learning goals for the current year?

Neglecting to account for the cost of the junk you're consuming can severely undermine your faith and clog your potential for joy and fulfillment. Excellence begets excellence. Put virtue in, and virtue comes out. There is no way to avoid it. Put weeds in, and weeds come out. There is no way to avoid this, either. It is the law of sowing and reaping. Remember the words of James Allen from his classic essay, "As a Man Thinketh": "Good thoughts and actions can never produce bad results; bad thoughts and actions can never produce good results."[3]

ACTIVATE 4:8 ::::::::::::::::::::::::::::::::

Drill #22

How could you be more intentional about what you feed your mind? On the following page, first identify a handful of mediocre or joy-decreasing inputs. Then, in the other column, list the productive, joy-producing inputs that you currently ingest or could consume going forward. At the bottom, indicate the first positive change you are willing to make.

JOY-DECREASING INPUTS

JOY-PRODUCING INPUTS

The Extra Mile

Organize a playlist of music that inspires you and fills you with joy beyond the norm. Listen to these tracks as much as possible over the remainder of the forty-day program, especially during the early morning hours and before going to bed at night.*

Make It Stick: Thought of the Day

I am a sponge!

Prayer

Lord, thank you for all the positive influences in my life. Guard my heart today and protect me from permitting black and white to gradually turn to gray. Amen.

---

*To download a FREE list of recommended music that corresponds with each chapter of this book, please visit the48principle.com.

WHAT DID YOU EAT FOR DINNER LAST NIGHT?

The Joy of Quality Questions

IMAGINE A SPARK from a campfire flying onto your sweater. What would you do? This happened to my son Brooks when he was about four years old. Quickly realizing what had happened, he panicked and started running toward me for help. In the rush, he tripped and almost fell into the fire, which would have created a legitimate problem. However, when he reached me, the spark had already self-extinguished. Even at the age of four, Brooks realized that he had overreacted.

As long as you quickly brush it away, a spark on your clothes will do no serious harm. The same is true of negative thoughts. When you train yourself to become aware of them, you can then sweep them away without much fanfare.

By now we know that the 4:8 Principle is about focusing on the good stuff. But since our lives are jam-packed with both positive developments and not-so-positive developments, how do we keep our thought lives pointed in the right direction?

How do we brush away the negative sparks that might otherwise interrupt our joy? How, specifically, do we go about focusing on the good stuff in the midst of the bad stuff?

Before I go any further, let me ask you an important question: What did you eat for dinner last night?

I often ask my clients this odd question for the express purpose of illustrating the power questions have to shift our attention from one thing to another. If you're stuck on a negative thought, you can displace it with a positive one.

It's all in how we frame things. For example, if I ask you, "What bothers you about your house?" you will, no doubt, share with me the features you dislike about your home. If I ask you, "What do you love the most about your house?" you will give me a very different response. Clearly, your answer will be determined by my question.

You'd never think of telling me what's great about your hometown if I asked you, "What stinks about where you live?" When we are thinking, we are really just asking and answering questions inside our heads. We are maintaining an inner conversation, asking and answering questions all day long. And when we enjoy a conversation with another person, the same process occurs, only with the added dynamic of someone else doing a portion of the asking.

What kinds of questions are you in the habit of asking yourself? I am more convinced than ever that the most effective technique for instilling the habit of 4:8 Thinking is instilling the habit of 4:8 Asking.

4:8 Asking = 4:8 Thinking

This means training yourself to habitually ask, re-ask, and then answer 4:8 Questions. Because questions instantly change what you are focusing on, they also, as a natural consequence, rapidly change how you feel. In fact, they are the single most effective tool for redirecting your attention from discouraging to encouraging, from hurtful to hopeful, from negative to positive.

So what exactly is a 4:8 Question? It's one that demands from you a positive response.

Here are some examples:

- What are four things I am grateful for right now?
- What are four of my most positive traits?
- What are four of my top achievements so far?
- Who are four people who love me the most?

Each of the questions above extracts a positive answer, and by asking for multiple answers to each, I am compelling you to dwell on the positive. To go even further, I could ask questions that engage you at a deeper level. Consider these, for example:

- What do I really love about my wife, and how could I express my appreciation today? (For a husband)
- In what ways could I take better care of myself this week and, as a result, take better care of my husband? (For a wife)
- What are my four best strengths, and how could I use them more often in the next week? (For all of us)

I open most of my workshops using 4:8 Questions similar to those above, and I recommend that you start your day with these questions as well. I answer these questions in the shower each morning; that way, they don't take any additional time. Many of my clients practice answering them with their families at dinnertime before grace. Other members of The 1% Club routinely cover these 4:8 Questions as they drift to sleep.

We all want to experience a fuller, deeper, more meaningful life. Who wouldn't want to be joy filled? But how do we actually reach that goal? It starts with a change of thinking. When you change the questions you consistently ask yourself, you start thinking differently. When you ask better questions, you receive better answers.

It is important to note that your supply of joy isn't compromised by any fleeting negative thought but rather by the negative thought that sets up shop in your mind and begins to spread, like a little spark could do to your sweater. After all, you cannot completely control the thoughts that are triggered from your surroundings, but you can unquestionably control what you choose to dwell on.

The 4:8 Questions are a simple tool to displace negativity in the short term and help you take conscious control of your repeated thoughts. Because of the way these questions are worded, they divert your attention away from the junk and toward the best things in life. You'll find that 4:8 Questions immediately change what you're focusing on. Consequently, they affect how you feel, as well as your level of creativity, excitement, and joy at any given moment.

Of course, you are free to ask questions that remind you of your mistakes, but why would you want to do that? Here are some examples of the negative stuff, presented as a friendly warning:

- What are the worst blunders I have ever made, and who was hurt as a consequence? How did this make me feel when it happened?

- What are four inevitable things that I am absolutely dreading in the next seven days?
- What are my most damaging weaknesses right now, and what trouble are they causing me?
- Who are four people who would really like to see me fail or suffer?

The enemy of your soul will nudge you to ask questions like those above. But since your thinking can only be as good as the questions you repeatedly ask, why not ask questions that direct your attention to the upside, not the downside? What do you like the most about this book so far?

ACTIVATE 4:8

Drill #23

What questions are you in the habit of asking yourself? On the following page, draft up to eight questions that trigger positive answers and shift your focus to the good things in life.

The Extra Mile

Using the questions developed in Drill #23 above, begin the habit of asking and answering these joy-generating questions while in the shower. Since you probably bathe regularly, this is an easy way to make good use of your mind without taking up any extra time. Alternatively, ask these questions during the first few minutes of your daily workout, or while you commute.

To turbo boost family joy, use these questions with your family at meals before saying grace and with your spouse before falling asleep at night. Keep 4:8 Questions at the top of your mind as much as possible throughout the day.

 Make It Stick: Thought of the Day

What am I thinking about right now?

Prayer

God, thanks for the gift of questions on which to focus my attention. Today, prompt me to ask questions that keep my mind focused on what is excellent and worthy of praise. Amen.

WHATEVER YOUR HAND FINDS TO DO

The Joy of Excellent Work

DO YOU BELIEVE God wants you to be joy filled?

Since you are reading this book, I am pretty sure I know how you answered that question. Here's another one: Can you imagine that God wants you to live with joy but merely tolerate what you do for a living? Do you believe God wants his children to be bored and miserable for half of their waking hours? I don't think so. Not any more than you would want your sons or daughters, week after week, to endure work that deflates and demotivates them. I have concluded that our work is part of *God's* plan for *our* joy.

Our work demands a significant portion of our lives here on the earth. God invented work because it is good for our souls. Work is not a punishment from God—in fact, it even existed before the fall of man. Genesis 2:15 says, "The LORD God took the man [Adam] and put him in the Garden of Eden to work it and take care of it" (NIV). Work is a gift from

God. This mind-set is the key to gaining joy from your work, not losing joy from your work. Imagine two almost identical individuals, living almost identical lives in the same town. The only difference is that one views his work as a necessary evil and the other as her calling. Is there any way that their respective outlooks do not influence their capacity for joy?

Accept that your work is your ministry; it is a platform that God leverages to help you grow spiritually. It is also one of the most significant stewardship opportunities you will ever experience. When you commit your work to God and yourself to excellence, you gain immense pleasure and satisfaction. You only have to observe his creation to see that God loves excellence.

The human heart beats forty million times a year with no days off. Although the human brain weighs only three or four pounds, it contains about one hundred billion neurons, which happens to be about the same number of stars as inhabit our galaxy. God made each individual person with the utmost precision.

Just look at our DNA. If transcribed into English, the DNA in a single human cell would fill a thousand-volume set of encyclopedias approximately six hundred pages each. The average adult carries about one hundred trillion cells in various sizes and shapes, with different functions and life expectancies. And consider that the moon is positioned just the right distance from the earth to control the tides and prevent us from needing a really big boat!

God made the world excellent, and he intended us for excellence as well. From Proverbs through the parables, God's Word shows he loves excellence, prudence, and productivity. Here's a sampling:

1. "In all labor there is profit, but idle chatter leads only to poverty" (Proverbs 14:23, NKJV).
2. "Whatever your hand finds to do, do it with your might" (Ecclesiastes 9:10, NKJV).
3. "Whether you eat or drink, or whatever you do, do all to the glory of God" (1 Corinthians 10:31, NKJV).
4. "Commit your actions to the LORD, and your plans will succeed" (Proverbs 16:3, NLT).
5. "Anyone who has been stealing must steal no longer, but must work, doing something useful with their own hands, that they may have something to share with those in need" (Ephesians 4:28, NIV).
6. "Lazy people take food in their hand but don't even lift it to their mouth" (Proverbs 26:15, NLT).
7. "Do you see a man who excels in his work? He will stand before kings" (Proverbs 22:29, NKJV).
8. "The plans of the diligent lead surely to plenty" (Proverbs 21:5, NKJV).
9. "Do not love sleep, lest you come to poverty" (Proverbs 20:13, NKJV).
10. "The desire of the lazy man kills him, for his hands refuse to labor" (Proverbs 21:25, NKJV).

In Scripture, excellence is both promoted and honored. Considering how much time will be absorbed in your vocation, can you think of a more vital area where your example can witness to others? Uncover the joy in your work. If you haven't already found it, it is usually just a quick attitude adjustment away. But if you can't discover it, create it. You essentially have two choices: either transition into work you love or, if this option is not immediately on the horizon, find ways to love what you currently are obliged to do.

Our work is not a secular activity but an extension of our walk with God. Unfortunately, too many believers, not to mention the rest of the population, still think of their work as a remote island, somehow isolated from their spiritual lives. Some even view work as a necessary evil, a kind of penance that must be paid so that they may better enjoy the evenings and weekends. This attitude does not glorify God, and it is not for you.

Whether you're a star athlete, a pastor, a business leader, an FBI agent, an entrepreneur, a stay-at-home mom, or a teacher, you have a marketplace. You have a group of people you are charged with serving in one way or another. It doesn't matter whether you work at home, in a factory, in your own business, or in a major corporate office. The object of the game is to serve others and add value to their businesses or lives. We are made to serve, and when we do so with excellence, we experience rich, lasting joy.

In everything, work as though God were your boss—for this is always the case. Your work carries eternal significance when you do it for the glory of God! And the way in which you do your work reveals your commitment to serve him in a real way. Cut yourself off from any alternative except complete excellence in your work.

Going the second mile and doing more than the minimum is a powerful key to abundant joy in your walk with God, your marriage, your health, your career, and all other areas of your life. So travel that lonely additional mile. Do far more than others expect. If you are in the business world, you'll find that doing more than you're paid for is the absolute fastest way to get paid more in the future.

The world argues, "Pay me more—then I'll work harder." But that's like sitting in front of the fireplace and saying, "Give me heat—then I'll put in the wood." To become great, first become a servant. Here's a quote that has really stuck with me ever since I first heard it about fifteen years ago: "If a man only does what is required of him, he is a slave. The moment he begins to do more than he is required, he becomes a free man."

To achieve excellence in the workplace and the joy that accompanies it, constantly seek new ways to grow your skills and fine-tune your talents. Remember, growth leads to joy; stagnation does not.

The apostle Paul makes a vivid comparison between the Christian lifestyle and the continuous training, preparation, and endurance necessary to compete in the ancient Olympic Games: "Do you not know that in a race all the runners run, but only one gets the prize? Run in such a way as to get the prize. Everyone who competes in the games goes into strict training. They do it to get a crown that will not last, but we do it to get a crown that will last forever" (1 Corinthians 9:24-25, NIV). Now that's a wonderful visual image. Plateaus are no fun and complacency never honors God, so challenge yourself to continually improve your work. Remember, "whether you eat or drink, or whatever you do, do all to the glory of God" (1 Corinthians 10:31, NKJV). You can accomplish more in one hour with God than in an entire lifetime without him. And, when you do, it will allow you, as King Solomon wrote, to "stand before kings" (Proverbs 22:29, NKJV).

ACTIVATE 4:8 :::::::::::::::::::::::::::::::::::::::

Drill #24

What could you do to increase your service and contribution to others in the marketplace? On the following page, identify up to four ways you could add more value to the people you work with and for, whether they are your employer or your customer. To the right, indicate the first step you could take to improving your service.

The Extra Mile

For the next eight days, emphasize the spiritual side of your work life as you never have before. Each day, rededicate your efforts to the Lord and recommit to excellence in all you do. Refuse to simply go through the motions. Instead, consistently remind yourself that you really report to God. Pray for partners, coworkers, clients, prospects, bosses, and vendors. Thank God for both current and future opportunities. For these eight days, make it a priority to bless with joy everyone you interact with all day long.

Make It Stick:
Thought of the Day

My work is my ministry!

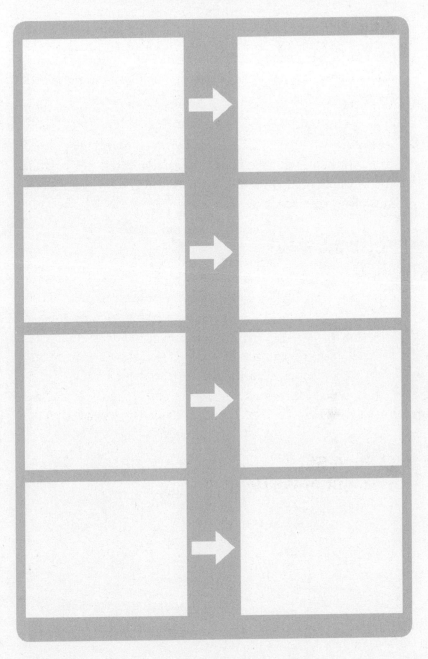

Prayer

Heavenly Father, thank you for the ministry of my work. Help me today to work with joy, deliver excellence, and set an example that glorifies you! Amen.

TO ADVANCE, FIRST RETREAT

The Joy of Reflection

FLYING THROUGH LIFE on autopilot can not only cause you to repeat both silly and serious mistakes; it can, with time, deprive you of joy. Fortunately, there is a life skill that helps switch off the default, robotic mind-set, freeing you to become more tuned in to how you are actually living your life. Then you can make changes—while there is still the time and relational goodwill to make them happen.

This life skill is simply called *reflection*. Merged with prayer and solitude, it supercharges spiritual growth and accelerates the development of wisdom. Best of all, the actual process is simple to implement. It consists of deliberately glancing back and grabbing the important lesson from the past in order to make better decisions in the future. The ancient Greeks saw a lot of wisdom in this. Socrates said, "The unexamined life is not worth living." Aristotle followed that observation with one of his own: "The unplanned life is not worth examining."

Today is the future we looked forward to ten years ago. But are we living with as much joy as we thought we would? Are we willing to question the choices we've made? Are we willing to evaluate how well we have managed our lives up until now? George Washington believed, "We ought not to look back, unless it is to derive useful lessons from past errors, and for the purpose of profiting by dear bought experience." That sums it up. Reflection is looking back in order to go forward with more wisdom—for the purpose of living more abundantly.

Due to the sheer velocity of life, few people regularly carve out time to evaluate the quality of their decisions and the direction of their lives. Even fewer work out a plan for their futures. Most people are swept along in the current of overloaded calendars and back-to-back activities for parent and child alike. Most just act, rinse, and then repeat the same habits day after day with very little thought to changing direction.

As a result of this frenetic pace, we develop dangerous blind spots, miss breakthrough opportunities, neglect irreplaceable relationships, and repeat mistakes. For most, reflection and introspection only follow a crisis, tragedy, or other significant emotional event. While reflection is certainly valuable in the aftermath of hardship, it's much more valuable when deployed proactively.

The Navy's Blue Angels pilots debrief after every show to make adjustments before the next day's demonstration begins. In football, the offense huddles, runs a play, reconvenes in the huddle, and runs the next play. Both the Blue Angels and football players watch videos of their performances to determine what went well and where they can improve. Videos add accountability; you can't hide from the film. After pinpointing mistakes, the succinct language used by Blue Angels to indicate a commitment to improvement is, "I'll fix it." These preplanned strategic pauses build wisdom, improve performance, and ultimately reduce stress.

Here are three simple questions that I've been using to challenge clients for more than twenty years. Simple as they are, these questions, asked and answered in seclusion with God, bring forth invaluable ideas that can and will steer our lives in joyful directions.

ONE: What has been working? Ask God to highlight what you are doing well. In evaluating any situation, relationship, or time frame, there are almost always some things that are working without a hitch. This is the joyful part! When reflecting, it's helpful to begin with the elements that are going well so that you keep a balanced perspective on the big picture.

TWO: What has not been working? This is the not-so-joyful part, at least for now. When we honestly assess any situation, we're able to identify at least a few things, large or small, that are giving us trouble or not progressing the way we'd like. Make sure to ask the Lord to illuminate any blind spots or other stubborn issues that could evade detection. It's important that we acknowledge where we are missing the mark or have a weak spot so we can ask God's forgiveness, if necessary, and correct our behavior before it happens again. Otherwise, the tendency is to keep doing things the same way indefinitely, and that certainly won't lead to more joy.

THREE: What do I need to improve? This is the most important of the three questions because it translates the feedback from the first two into positive forward action. In light of your assessment of what's working and what's not, what do you need to do differently? Pray for God to give you sensitivity to his will and show you clearly what to do next. How should you change your approach or modify your strategy so that you experience noticeably better results in the future?

You can benefit from these three questions in many different situations. You can use them at the end of the year, quarter, month, week, or day. When you debrief a whole year or quarter, you invest more time and thought than when you debrief a week, but the concept is the same.

You can also use these questions to improve your performance after a meeting, a conversation, a date, or even a golf shot. These are certainly valuable questions to share with your children because they force critical thinking and expand wisdom. Children and teenagers can learn to do a sixty-second debrief of the important situations and activities they are involved in.

Reflection can also be a significant tool in our spiritual lives. If you want to advance your relationship with God and experience more joy, you will find it very helpful to set aside extended periods of listening time with God—maybe on a weekly or monthly basis. In the same way that strong, earthly relationships are built through attentive love and listening, we must do the same to grow our relationships with God.

Deliberately block out time in your calendar for withdrawing from the constant busyness of life. Find a peaceful spot where you can be free of distractions, where your mind can become still and relaxed. Then simply become lost in the awesomeness of God. Read some psalms that describe God and his character. Remind yourself of what you know to be true about God—his boundless love, his unfathomable wisdom, his limitless power, and his incredible grace. Then just listen. No rush, no hurry. Just listen. When your mind is centered on the

Lord, ask your reflection questions. What is working in your spiritual walk? How are you becoming more and more like Christ? What is not working? What changes could you make to become more open to God's transformation in your life?

How much time you take will depend upon your purpose, but whether it's an hour or an entire afternoon or a full day, it will be a most valuable use of your time. To advance in life, first retreat with God.

ACTIVATE 4:8 :::::::::::::::::::::::::::::::

Drill #25

Complete a quick reflection exercise on the following page. Building on today's lesson, first identify what has been working well in your life over the last ninety days. Include all areas of your life, such as finances, interpersonal relationships, work, health, family, church, or home. Next, list what has *not* been working so well. Below, jot down a couple of things you could do in the upcoming ninety days to improve yourself.

The Extra Mile

Set aside fifteen minutes to a half hour once per week to debrief the previous seven days. Identify progress and setbacks over the last week, and ask God to illuminate your understanding and direct your actions over the upcoming week. For added influence, include similar reflection periods with your spouse, kids, and colleagues at work.

Make It Stick: Thought of the Day

> I glance back and move forward with wisdom!

Prayer

Heavenly Father, thanks for the insight that comes from consistently evaluating my life. Help me to pause today and reflect on the person I am becoming. Amen.

DAY
26

STOP AND DROP

The Joy of Restraint

JUST DROP IT!

At any given moment, we are either on an upward or a downward emotional spiral. Rarely are we emotionally flat, not trending one way or the other. But when we get drawn into a negative spiral, we have a key decision to make. We can overreact and kick off a self-defeating reaction cycle, or we can simply drop the negative thought.

You can refuse to indulge negative thoughts. You can refuse to rehash them, replay them, or otherwise foster them—and you will benefit. When you neglect to drop the negative thought, you are choosing to drink the poison. Ironically, when you spew emotional venom toward another person, either verbally or silently, you are the one who receives the stiffest dose. As unfair as this seems to be, it is a sobering truth. Whatever you express to others is impressed on yourself.

Instead of enabling negative thoughts to affect you, you

can starve them by letting them go. You already have plenty of experience doing this. Let me explain.

Have you ever experienced a distracting thought when you were in the middle of a business meeting or perhaps a romantic dinner with your spouse? Maybe you thought about an e-mail you needed to return or about the morning carpool plans. Quickly realizing that the thought was inappropriate, you just dropped it and continued with your evening.

Many times I've been at the movies with my family and had certain obligations or "to dos" pop into my mind. I tell myself, *This isn't the time. I can deal with that on Monday.* That little conversation almost instantly releases the distracting thought. You've done exactly the same thing on many occasions because you thought it was the right thing to do. In fact, you are constantly switching mental gears, but this switching happens largely as a reflex, not as a deliberate intention. A number of years ago I was in the middle of a little squabble with my wife when we heard our four-year-old falling out of his bed with a loud thud, closely followed by an unforgettable cry. Immediately we halted the negativity and turned our attention to our child, thereby inadvertently activating the Law of Exchange—replacing one thought with another. We are free to do that anytime we choose.

We sometimes seem to think we have a right to negative thoughts. Instead of dismissing them, we embrace them. There's no benefit to doing that. You can drop the thoughts anytime you want; in fact, I'm giving you permission to do so! As one of my mentors shared with me years ago, "That thought is not attached to you, Tommy; it's not glued to you. It is no more real than the dream you had last night." It's merely the power of habit that causes us to latch on to the negative and drop the positive. It doesn't have to be this way.

Many people don't want to hear this because they have become accustomed to venting their negativity to another person. Some people advocate venting because it lets off negative steam that has been mounting. But this cathartic benefit is often mitigated by the unintended consequence of the steam spreading to another person—usually someone they really care about.

At best, the therapeutic benefit of venting is short lived. The negative emotion that was supposedly released often rears its ugly head once again when prompted by a new event. At worst, an important relationship is damaged without addressing the real source of the negativity. If you have to vent, then vent by hand in a journal. That way, when you let off steam, it won't affect anyone else.

What about venting brings such relief? Once a person vents, he or she drops the negative thought and feels satisfied. But is venting a necessary prerequisite to dropping the thought, or could the drama of venting be bypassed? Maybe the venting is just a learned, popular ritual that helps us dump negative thoughts. What if you could break the link at the beginning? You could say, "It's not worth it." You could say, "I am responsible." Or you could give the other person the benefit of the doubt.

As long as you are going to drop the thought eventually, why not drop it at the start, relax a little, and avoid damaging a relationship? It's worth thinking about. All it takes is a little cool-headed forethought, blended with a touch of self-discipline. Decide in advance to make this your personal mode of operation. When you drop a negative thought, you preempt an emotional eruption. This is a good thing!

By catching negativity early, you keep yourself in a resource-ful state of mind, giving yourself the best shot at effectively solving problems, dealing with stress, overcoming challenges, and generating more joy.

ACTIVATE 4:8

Drill #26

In this drill, I want you to weigh the pros and cons of dropping negative thoughts before they metamorphose into full-blown negative emotions. In the column on the left, list all the reasons for either harboring or venting negative thoughts. On the other side, identify the reasons to drop negative thoughts before they erupt. At the bottom, indicate your preference for dealing with negative thoughts going forward.

The Extra Mile

Rehearse what it could be like to simply "drop the thought." This visualization will help you become accustomed to this very healthy practice. By yourself, get comfortable and relaxed by taking several deep breaths. Then imagine a common upset-ting scenario, but instead of fueling this situation negatively, see yourself simply dropping the irritating thought and moving on with whatever you were doing. Dropping the thought doesn't mean that your impression of the situation is wrong, but it prevents the circumstances from escalating. If the issue merits revisiting, you can always do so when the dust has settled and you are emotionally sober.

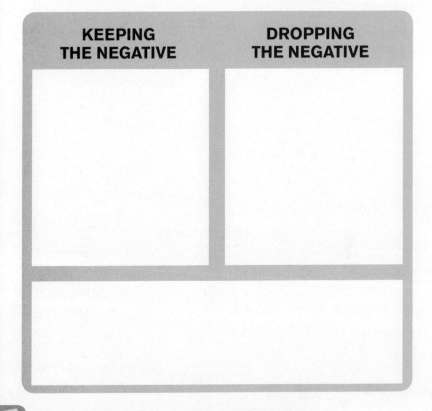

KEEPING THE NEGATIVE	DROPPING THE NEGATIVE

Make It Stick: Thought of the Day

I automatically disrupt destructive thoughts.

Prayer

Heavenly Father, thank you for the amazing influence of joyful think-ing. Prod me today to simply drop those thoughts that threaten my joy. Amen.

DON'T SWEAT THE BIG STUFF, EITHER

The Joy of Conquering Mountains

THERE IS ENORMOUS positive power in adversity. Wouldn't it be great if you really believed that? Well, it's true. Adversity is what molds our character. As James teaches us in the New Testament, "Count it all joy when you fall into various trials, knowing that the testing of your faith produces patience" (James 1:2-3, NKJV). Trying to avoid adversity is like trying to avoid life. If you are somehow able to hide from adversity, you are unlikely to really be living.

With God's help, though, there's no need to get stressed and bent out of shape, even over the big stuff in life. It may take a little practice, but it is possible to retain your joy even in the midst of life's inevitable hardships. And with more poise and calm, you will do a much better job of responding to the difficulty, whatever it may be.

We have all experienced slumps, setbacks, and seasons spent in the desert. (And if we haven't yet, we will.) We experience negative stress when we feel out of control of the events in our lives. It's like being in a fast-moving car without a steering wheel. We experience stress when we live inconsistently with biblical principles. Most of all, we experience stress when we don't sense God's presence or are not following his will for our lives.

But if we never had tough times, we would never appreciate the great times. What would triumph mean if it were not partnered with strain and struggle? We often expend so much energy trying to avoid adversity that when it finally comes, we're too exhausted to deal with it creatively. But adversity develops our character, just as weight training develops our muscles. Neither is particularly enjoyable when we're in the middle of it, but both can produce great results.

Weight training speeds up our metabolism and makes us look and feel better. It makes us stronger and more resilient in the face of accidents and all sorts of trauma. Our physical muscles become stronger when confronted with resistance, and the same is true for the "muscles" in our mind, spirit, and character.

Character is built by adversity, but strong character is not the inevitable result of adversity. It all depends on how we choose to respond to the circumstances of life. Setbacks and struggles can shape us into something exceptional or something entirely unremarkable. It's how we respond to the difficulty and what we learn from it that upgrades our character.

James Allen explains, "The outer world of circumstance shapes itself to the inner world of thought, and both pleasant and unpleasant external conditions are factors which make for the ultimate good of the individual. As the reaper of his own harvest, man learns both by suffering and bliss."[4]

We must understand that maintaining our joy has a lot to do with mitigating the downside of human nature. Character flaws are like cracks in the foundation of an otherwise solid structure. They may look small, but eventually they will cause significant damage. The more we compromise our values, the more our standards shrink.

Our character is the essence of who we are. It's the sum total of our thoughts and habits, our vices and virtues. Yet character isn't part of our DNA. Rather, it's something that develops throughout our lives with every choice we make. Helen Keller said, "Character cannot be developed in ease and quiet. Only through experience of trial and suffering can the soul be strengthened, vision cleared, ambitions inspired and success achieved."

We never quite know what we are made of until we are put through the fire. Just as a pressed orange never yields apple juice, nothing comes out of people under stress unless it's already a part of who they are. When you face difficulties, take a close look at how you respond. What do your reactions say about your character?

Adversity comes in all shapes and sizes, and it has many names: failure, tragedy, difficulty, obstacle, setback, crisis, or suffering. Regardless of what you call it, adversity plays no favorites and may strike with equal vengeance upon your business, your marriage, your health, your family, or any other corner of your life. According to Goethe, "Character develops itself in the full stream of life."

Consider for a moment that the biggest problem you are now facing might be exactly what you need to chisel your character so that you become perfectly prepared to follow God's path for your life. As you deal with trials, look for the lesson, the wisdom, the opportunity, or any other blessing that could transform the entire situation into something productive and valuable.

Interpreting adversity as a strength builder drains much of the negative energy out of it. When you view adversity as an ally, it begins to benefit you in unforeseen ways. Remember, the presence of tension, conflict, and difficulty indicates that growth is trying to take place. When you view this adversity as natural, normal, and, in fact, even necessary, it empowers you to take advantage of its potential for growth.

How do you tend to deal with adversity? How have you coped with difficulty and misfortune in the past? What happens when you are under fire and feeling the stinging punch of stressful situations? Adversity, regardless of its origin, can be turned to your advantage when you trust God to be bigger, stronger, and more tenacious than anything you ever face.

You can discover the treasure within the trouble, but you must train yourself to look for it! Times may be tough now, and these new challenges can either defeat you or inspire you. They will either tear you down or build you up. As Alexander Graham Bell wrote, "When one door closes, another opens; but we often look so regretfully upon the closed door that we do not see the one that has opened for us." Affirm your ability, with God's help, to convert all difficult circumstances to your advantage and his glory. Remember, don't sweat the big stuff, either!

ACTIVATE 4:8

Drill #27

Identify three instances of adversity in your life and what you learned from each, either during the situation or later. Then, at the bottom, note the advice you would pass on to a teenager about the purpose of adversity and how to deal with it wisely and gracefully.

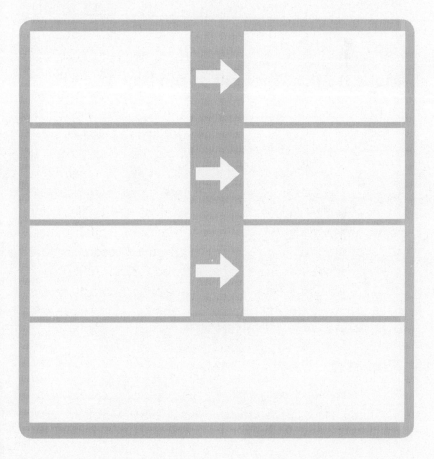

The Extra Mile

Create a one-page game plan for dealing with future adversity. Instead of waiting until the heat of the moment when you might not be thinking so clearly, be proactive and think ahead. What is the first thing you will do when intimidating problems surface? What will you do next? What questions will you ask yourself? With whom will you seek counsel? None of us will be free of difficulties on this earth, so it is best to consider how we will deal with them when they hit. Once your plan is ready to go, put it away. The mental work is complete.

Make It Stick: Thought of the Day

I get back up again!

Prayer

Lord, thank you for being with me, especially in the midst of adversity. Today, show me what you want me to learn and how you want me to grow, both from my triumphs and my troubles. Amen.

WORDS OF MASS DESTRUCTION

The Joy of Speaking Life

NOTHING GETS IN THE WAY of our joy more than our mouths.

The words we speak to ourselves can wreak havoc throughout our lives. The Bible is clear that our manner of speech either enlarges our joy or narrows it. After all, in Proverbs 18:21 we are advised that both life and death are in the power of the tongue. The words you mutter to yourself have the power to encourage or discourage, to motivate or deflate, to generate joy or repel it. In Ephesians 4:29, Paul tells us, "Do not let any unwholesome talk come out of your mouths, but only what is helpful for building others up according to their needs, that it may benefit those who listen" (NIV).

Disregarding this advice, most people routinely say unwholesome, 8:4 things to or about themselves that they would never say to a respected friend. Here are a few examples:

1. I'm never going to be that happy again.
2. We're just growing apart.
3. I hate the way I look.
4. How could he forgive me?
5. I don't have what it takes.
6. The honeymoon is officially over.
7. Where did all my energy go?
8. I'm just not creative.

Have you ever said junk-producing comments like this to yourself or heard somebody else say them? When you think careless thoughts, and especially when you speak careless words, you can count on losing some joy.

Fortunately, you are not limited to thinking or speaking in only one way. You can choose from an infinite number of positive possibilities. So refuse to give airtime to these kinds of joy-sabotaging thoughts, which are obviously in stiff opposition to who God wants you to be. Stop beating up on yourself—starting right now.

Instead, speak to and about yourself as if you've already fulfilled your highest potential. Speak confidently about your life as if God had assured you of a wondrous future—because he has! Be a respectful and encouraging friend to yourself. Use your words to lift up others and expand your joy. Like love, the more joy you give, the more you get to keep for yourself.

In today's lesson, I want to encourage you to take charge of your mouth for the purpose of disciplining your mind. Understand that much mental mayhem is advanced by sloppy speech. The words we speak both reflect our inner beliefs and simultaneously reinforce those beliefs. If we speak the truth, this is good. If we speak untruth, this is bad. Careless words corrupt our joy. Faithful words fuel our joy.

Imagine you've got a microphone hanging around your neck, and every word you speak to yourself today will be recorded and played back on national television tomorrow. Additionally, the transcript will be posted on Facebook and continually Tweeted. Would this be a good thing?

Would your speech more likely represent the problems of the present, or your hopes for the future? Would your words emphasize your blessings, or your worries? Would your words accurately reflect your faith in God? Many pray and subsequently speak as if they assume their prayers will go unanswered. Their prayers and ensuing conversations oppose each other. After praying, they continue to verbalize fears and worries as if God had commanded their troubles to be permanent. Why not assume the best-case scenario and then discipline your mouth to match your faith?

How about you? Imagine yesterday's words were recorded. Would you be pleased with your example to the world? Would your words draw more people to the Lord, or steer them in an alternate direction?

Although you may not have an actual microphone, your words are being recorded in your subconscious and will be played back at a time of its choosing, influencing your future perceptions and decisions.

When you use your mouth to argue for your limitations, you get to keep them. But changing the way you communicate with yourself alters your self-concept. The words you use today will create the world you'll experience tomorrow. Depending on your focus, that is either a great problem or a great opportunity.

Become aware of your words. When someone asks how you are doing, how do you answer? Do you give the standard "fine" or "okay"? Why not use that everyday question as an opportunity to claim your joy? Reply, "I'm terrific!" or "Excellent, thanks!" or "I'm fantastic."

Why? First of all, compared to millions if not billions of people in the world who struggle to meet the most basic needs, you *are* doing great. Second, your answer acts as a command to your subconscious. If you want an average day, then answer, "Fine, thanks." If you want something more, then avoid the boring, joy-snuffing replies. Remember, the potential for joy is within you, but it is up to you to release it.

Begin today to speak only what you seek, as if you are *already* the person God intends for you to become and are *already* living the life of your dreams. Speak as if you believe in your prayers. Stop clinging to the past by talking about yourself as the person you no longer desire to be. Avoid making repeated references to your mistakes and fears. Reflect for a moment on Isaiah 43:18-19: "Forget the former things; do not dwell on the past. See, I am doing a new thing! Now it springs up; do you not perceive it? I am making a way in the wilderness and streams in the wasteland" (NIV).

Become highly sensitive to what you think about most often. What you say to yourself and others provides the biggest clue about the quality of your thought life.

Remind yourself that nothing is too good to be true for a child of the King. God wants you to prosper and have every good thing. Do not block his generosity with unprofitable talk. Swap all self-defeating words, phrases, and expressions with their positive opposites. Then practice using the 4:8 Principle in almost any situation:

- on the phone
- when you text
- when you post something on Facebook
- with your family
- with your coworkers
- with friends
- at social events

Talk only about what is "good, pure, lovely, and worthy of praise." Avoid saying things that are unbecoming of a child of God. Make everything that comes out of your mouth first pass through the filter of Philippians 4:8. If you cannot say something positive, silence is the best substitute.

With persistence, you can control your tongue. Align your words with your prayers. Agree with God. Train your mind via your mouth. Cut out, one by one, every expression or remark that is inconsistent with the person he wants you to be. You can do it!

ACTIVATE 4:8

Drill #28

It's one thing for other people to fill us with junk. It is even worse when we choose to feed ourselves toxic thoughts. In today's drill (found on the following page), list up to four limiting or critical things you have said to yourself more than once. In the corresponding space to the right, write the positive opposite. Then ask God to reveal which thought is closer to the truth.

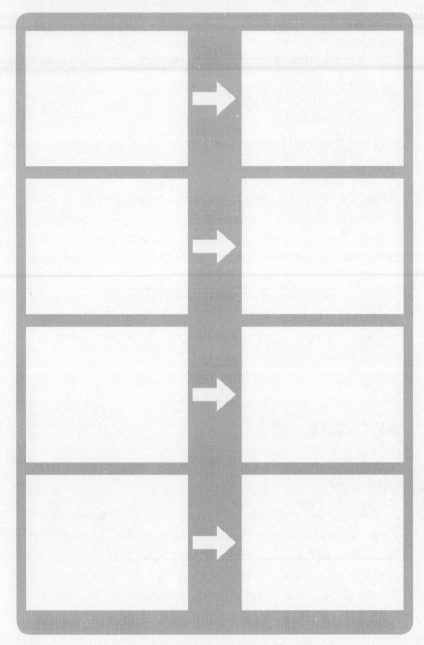

The Extra Mile

Ask one trusted friend and one family member to point out when you verbally disagree with God and speak self-defeating words. Make notes of your tendencies based on their feedback. Give them permission to hold you accountable to your best self. This heightened awareness will help you more effectively train your mind through your words.

Make It Stick: Thought of the Day

> I release joy through my words!

Prayer

God, thanks for the power you've given me to speak life and spread joy. Today, help me align my words with my prayers. Amen.

WAY TO GO!

The Joy of Other People's Success

YOUR SUCCESS blesses others. Other people's success blesses you. This is part of God's miraculous and perfect design! Just as you want your children to be successful, God wants each of us to succeed, provided that our definition of success is right. God wants us to reach our potential and contribute to the world in tremendous ways.

You and I, as well as everyone we know, can become successful without anyone else suffering setbacks, harm, or downturns. God didn't create us to profit at the expense of one another. Can we imagine our all-loving, all-wise heavenly Father designing a world where one individual's gain triggers another individual's loss?

The truth is that everyone can fulfill his or her potential with no one else being cheated in the slightest. God's success system makes room for everyone to shine brightly. Only the architect of the universe could author such a perfect system! Our success truly does bless others.

For individuals, success is the ongoing process of making God's desires our desires, becoming today a little more like the person he engineered us to be. Collectively, success is God's way of proliferating abundance. God uses our success to help others while we help ourselves. When we do well (in our area of charge), we are better able to do good (in the world at large).

We don't succeed at the expense of others but in service to others. Success is a multiplier, not a divider as is promoted in certain circles today. Authentic success spills over to benefit many beyond the minority who courageously planted the first seeds and jump-started the process.

To examine this in a bit more detail, let's look at one example of how a single entrepreneur's financial success blesses many. To begin with, that entrepreneur creates a job—two, if you include his own. His employee uses her salary to put a down payment on her first home. As a result, two real-estate agents earn a commission. That enables one of the agents to pay off his credit-card debt, allowing him to live responsibly and enjoy peace of mind. The other agent is able to take a long-awaited vacation to Hawaii with her husband.

As a result of this trip to Hawaii, the airline generates revenue, along with the Hawaiian hotels, restaurants, attractions, and rental-car companies. Additionally, a teenager earns a little spending money house-sitting while the couple is traveling. With the extra spending cash, the teenager takes his girlfriend out for a nice dinner, making money for the restaurant owner and earning a tip for the server.

With the additional profit from this and other customers, the restaurant owner can hire a manager so that she can have more time to spend with her family and to concentrate on growing the business. With his tips, the server can pay for gas on the way home and buy some flowers for his wife. The wife benefits, the owner of the gas station benefits, the oil company benefits, the local and state governments that collect tax benefit, and so on.

Now multiply this by one hundred, by one thousand, or by one hundred thousand. Consider Hobby Lobby's founder and CEO, David Green, who is responsible for sixteen thousand jobs. Or how about Bernie Marcus and Arthur Blank, who together via Home Depot have created more than three hundred thousand jobs? The value created in the marketplace by the individuals who take the initiative, risk their own futures, and pour their hearts into serving others in the free marketplace creates massive blessings for all of us. We should rejoice in this!

This success cascade repeats itself perpetually, not only in the business world, but in all walks of life. From schoolteachers and ministers to surgeons and salespeople, when we serve others in excellence, a ripple effect of blessing spreads far and wide. How does this dynamic present itself in your line of work?

Not only does God want us to succeed, he also wants us to cheer when our brothers and sisters succeed. I teach my kids to appreciate other people's success, whether I like the person or not. I certainly try to highlight those with the highest moral character, but I honor all those who have accomplished something meaningful.

I also try to promote the various expressions of success: the nurse, the small-business owner, the Olympic athlete, the corporate CEO, the homemaker, the inventor, the minister, and the famous actor—to mention but a few. If the aforementioned individuals have a goal and are serving others in some decent or principled way in order to reach that goal, I consider them successful and I am proud of them, even though I probably don't know them personally.

Too many people today drag others down with their sour-grapes attitude, attempting to minimize others' victories by attributing their success to cheating, luck, or some other petti-ness. But this spite seldom hurts the target of the resentment. Instead, it only hurts the possessor of it, smothering the joy that comes from sharing in the blessings of fellow human beings. Don't fall into this trap.

Instead, be much bigger than that. If you'd be proud of your son or daughter for accomplishing some feat, celebrate anyone else who does something similar. We need more peo-ple serving, giving, creating, innovating, and leading. There is plenty of opportunity to go around.

Work to become genuinely happy for others when they succeed, get promoted, or win the top prize. Sharing, even vicariously, in the good fortune or hard-fought success of others not only makes you a good sport; it assures you of far more joy. Send texts, e-mails, or handwritten notes of congratulations to friends, acquaintances, and strangers alike when they win or accomplish something noteworthy.

If you are secure in God's love, you know that he has a plan for you, and you are not threatened by others' talents or successes. Applaud what God is doing through others, because whatever he accomplishes in their lives, he can accomplish in yours also. Think and speak positive things about other people when they succeed. This helps release those gifts in you as well.

If you would like to have greater financial rewards tomorrow, then start appreciating those who are already experiencing that kind of success today. Pay attention to how they are thinking, earning, investing, saving, spending, and otherwise behaving differently than you are. Be on the lookout for the lessons their success is leaving behind. I hold no ill will toward other authors who have sold more books than I have. To the contrary, I admire them, look up to them, and want to learn from them.

When you see someone get the promotion that you wanted, it can be a real bummer. Difficult as it is, thank God for the other person's success. Not only does this practice—and I emphasize *practice* because it does not always come naturally—save your joy; it fine-tunes your attitude. It helps you become more receptive to the very breakthrough you are praying for.

One of the best things we can do to overcome envy or jealousy is to pray for others to be blessed in the way we desire to be blessed. It's the ultimate application of the Golden Rule.

If you want to have a stronger marriage, pray wholeheartedly for those you know who are striving for the same progress. And when you see couples experiencing the kind of relationship you desire, thank God for that and pray that he continues to bless them, that their marriage glorifies him, and that yours does as well. For the sake of your joy, if nothing else, ask God to free you of envy and jealousy.

There is always going to be someone we know who has something better than we do, whether it is physical appearance, formal education, house, social status, talent, career, or marriage. If you desire it for yourself, then love it, appreciate it, and admire it wherever it exists, even when you spot it in someone else's life. This positive recognition seems to hit a mental switch that releases all resistance to living the life of our dreams.

God loves us all equally, and this is why he created us in his likeness, despite our individual differences. Sameness doesn't appear to be part of his plan. We have different roles to fulfill and different missions to accomplish. And, just maybe, God is more interested in our spiritual equity than our material equality. Let's trust him to bring us just what we need to help us become closer and closer to the person he created us to be.

Remember, your success blesses others.

ACTIVATE 4:8

Drill #29

In today's drill, identify three successful individuals. Alongside each, write what you appreciate about them or their results. In the third column, identify a few people (or groups of people) who have directly or indirectly benefited from their success.

The Extra Mile

Identify two or three individuals with ambitions similar to yours, and commit to praying for their success for the next eleven days. Invite other like-minded friends and family members to do the same. Share the truth that "your success blesses others"!

PERSON	CHARACTERISTICS	BENEFICIARIES

Make It Stick: Thought of the Day

> When other people do well, it brings me joy.

Prayer

Heavenly Father, thank you for the inspiration and blessing of other people's success. Help me today to cheer the great things you are doing through others! Amen.

AFFIRMING GOD'S GOODNESS

The Joy of Telling the Truth

THOSE OF YOU who have read *The 4:8 Principle* may remember my son Mason and his affinity for demolition. Nothing illustrates the ups and downs of human nature quite as well as a rambunctious toddler and a box of Legos. When Mason was about three years old, we would spend a lot of time together building things. He especially liked building Lego towers because the potential for new and different designs was limited only by his imagination (and the number of pieces in the set). One afternoon, we began the construction process with Mason in charge and closely supervising every piece I put in place.

Pretty impressed with the progress of the building, I glanced at Mason and noticed a rather mischievous look in his eye—which was quickly followed by a sweeping karate chop straight through the center of our efforts of the last fifteen minutes. Of course this demolished our tower, but it produced great laughter in both of us. Seconds after destroying our first structure, Mason was quickly picking up the pieces and beginning to assemble building number two. This process of building and tearing down continued for some time.

Our spiritual growth and development often mirrors this toddler-style fun. We make great strides toward our goals, only to wreck that progress with self-inflicted sabotage, forcing us to start again. The wrecking ball may take different forms—negative self-talk, fear, neglect, procrastination, worry, and so forth—but its effects can be devastating. Often what we really need is to get out of our own way. We have to stop tearing ourselves down and start building ourselves up. One highly effective way we can do that is through affirming the good things in our lives.

An affirmation is a joy tool that helps you build your character, your personality, your attitude—in fact, your very existence here on earth. Think of each affirmation as a positive mental vitamin or "thought conditioner." By affirming what you hope for and pray for, you strengthen the belief that its attainment is imminent. The words you use are like seeds that, once planted, begin to shape the world you see. King Solomon wrote, "Words kill, words give life; they're either poison or fruit—you choose" (Proverbs 18:21, *The Message*). Whether you realize it or not, you are always affirming something because you are always thinking. More accurately, you are constantly either building or demolishing.

The key questions are, What are you affirming? Would you be affirming the same thing if God were physically standing next to you, encouraging you?

Most of us are erratic with our thoughts. We downgrade our potential by thinking first one thing, then another—thinking of God's grace, then feeling guilty about sins we have already confessed; thinking of God's awesome power, then talking about how we cannot seem to get rid of some little virus. We think about God's provision and then seconds later worry over the bills.

Imagine getting in a taxi at the airport and telling the driver to take you downtown. Moments later, you ask him to return to the airport. Following your instructions, he turns around, but then you direct him back downtown again. If this actually happened, the driver would likely kick you out on the side of the road, with no net progress to report.

We are often like a driver frantically shifting from drive to reverse, to drive and back to reverse, with no hope of moving very far ahead. This barrage of mental contradictions locks us into whatever behavior has already become entrenched as a habit. Try as we might to change our outward actions, we soon return to the behavior triggered from the inside. It does not have to be this way.

When we affirm God's goodness, we declare with conviction the love, abundance, and joy that God has promised his children. Refuse to claim anything that you don't want in your life, such as *my* cold, *my* headache, *my* bad back, *my* debt, or *my* troubles. Instead, attach yourself mentally and verbally to what you *do* want, such as joy, peace, fun, prosperity, significance, and excellent health.

Escape from conversations involving cynicism, doubt, fear, worry, or gossip. Typically, self-talk refers to your habitual inner voice, which becomes evident to others when you speak. As a rule, it is quite contagious. And just as you might cringe on an airplane when you hear coughing, sneezing, or other signs of sickness nearby, you should stay alert to the negativity of those around you.

Do not let others contaminate your mind with their pessimism and idle words. Practically speaking, this means talking to yourself and others only about the conditions you desire and the things God wants for you. We can look to Scripture for some examples of what God promises:

- He can do more than we ask or imagine (Ephesians 3:20).
- Those who seek him lack no good thing (Psalm 34:10).
- Nothing can ever separate us from the love of God (Romans 8:38-39).
- Jesus will be with us always (Matthew 28:20).

When we affirm those things in our lives, we are speaking in faith and using meaningful words. In Matthew 12:37, Jesus teaches, "By your words you will be justified, and by your words you will be condemned" (NKJV). We are responsible for what we say.

To affirm simply means to build up or reinforce that which you want and expect in your life. An affirmation is the perfect expression of faith. Practicing affirmations retrains your automatic self-talk so that it is in harmony with a joy-filled life. Affirmations alert your mind to the blessings that God has already poured into your life.

ACTIVATE 4:8 :::::::::::::::::::::::::::::::

Drill #30

In the space provided below, write—as if explaining to some-one who doesn't share your faith—four promises of God that bring a joyful smile to your face.

- _____

_____

_____

- _____

_____

_____

- _____

_____

_____

- _____

_____

_____

The Extra Mile

Handwrite separately onto 3 x 5 cards your eight favorite promises from God pulled straight from the Bible. Keep these cards in your car, laptop case, or purse to review often, especially during unexpected spare moments. Make a second copy of this same list on sticky notes and place in strategic locations around your house.

Make It Stick: Thought of the Day

The words I use shape the world I see!

Prayer

Father, thank you for the blessings I have and the blessings I am receiving. Help me this day to affirm your goodness with my thoughts, words, and deeds. Amen.

DAY
31

MOTION RULES EMOTION

The Joy of Self-Discipline

SELF-DISCIPLINE is an acquired virtue that directs our appetite and passions in a productive, joy-producing direction. Self-discipline occurs in the moments when intention defeats indulgence, when mission trumps mood, and when spirit conquers sentiment.

Those who are undisciplined, however, are slaves to their feelings, a condition that squashes joy and causes all sorts of trouble throughout one's life. What happens when someone is a slave to emotions? If a man feels like exercising, he will. If he doesn't, he won't. If a mom feels like having that important conversation with her teenager, she will. If she doesn't, she won't. Whatever a person is feeling at a given moment becomes the guiding force.

Disciplining ourselves to override unproductive emotions opens up a whole new universe of possibilities and will elevate both our joy and our success in all areas of life. As William

James wrote, "Action seems to follow feeling, but really action and feeling go together; and by regulating the action, which is under the more direct control of the will, we can indirectly regulate the feeling, which is not."[5]

I teach my clients that there is a considerable difference between what we *can't* do and what we *won't* do to improve our current circumstances. *Can't* is about legitimate capability, and *won't* is about emotional willingness. Lots of people toss their bad habits in the "can't pile" when they really belong in the "won't pile," and it can cost them dearly.

People in financial trouble tell themselves they can't downgrade their lifestyle when they really mean they won't. Many spouses tell themselves they can't do what it takes to strengthen or save their marriage, when they really mean they won't. Once we've mentally assigned a productive behavior to the "can't pile," we tend to act helpless and don't exert any self-discipline toward resurrecting it. The fog and haze of raw emotion can inflict inexpressible damage.

Although we live in an instant culture where "now" is no longer fast enough, self-discipline equips us to keep our impulsivity and desire for instant satisfaction in check. We sacrifice something lesser today for something greater tomorrow. This is the great promise.

There is no law mandating that our decisions must originate with our feelings. This is good news because when feelings are allowed to control the will, a train wreck is never far away. Consider the mental process of a man who commits adultery. Does he use his reason to evaluate the circumstances, pray for wisdom and guidance, and then, with clear conscience, make a sound decision to violate his covenant with God and his pledge to his wife? Hardly! Certainly, all reason and conscience were temporarily suspended to satisfy passionate feelings in the heat of the moment. Very likely, those amplified feelings were fueled by sustained inappropriate thoughts (RATs) that preceded the adulterous occurrence. This man was clearly drunk with emotion, submissive to his feelings. And this can happen to all of us in far less dramatic circumstances.

One of the most effective and least utilized methods for upgrading your emotional life is acting your way into the feelings you most desire. If you're not experiencing as much joy, passion, or satisfaction as you would like, you can, over time, act your way into those higher emotions by behaving and thinking consistently with your future emotional goal. If you believe God has great plans for your life, then that belief, if it is true, must translate into incredible enthusiasm and joy. How could it not? Assume the mood you would have if your greatest goal had already been achieved or your number one prayer request had been answered.

Most people resist this option because they have been conditioned to believe that positive emotions should happen naturally. Thanks to lots of cultural conditioning, many conclude that if it's not automatic, it's not authentic. From time to time audience members will share with me that they felt like they were being phony or lying to themselves when they acted more positively than they actually felt at the moment.

I can understand these reactions, but one thing is certain: if you rule out acting your way into your feelings, you will forever be doomed to enjoy only those positive emotions that arise spontaneously. However, once you've decided that following Scripture and fulfilling your full potential dictates a particular choice, then "acting your way into feelings" is simply the discipline that aligns your behavior with your values. Most of us face these mini defining moments all day long. With our most important relationships, we choose to go all out or merely go through the motions, to serve or to be selfish, to initiate progress or to wait for the other person, all based on how we happen to feel at a particular moment.

God has built this power for personal change into all of us, even though it may not feel comfortable right away. Any new behavior feels a bit unnatural until we grow accustomed to it. To those who feel as if they're lying when they act better than they feel, let me say that there is a far greater likelihood that their negative emotions, not their positive ones, are rooted in untruth. Have you ever been completely worn out, but miraculously revived by an invitation to do something you love? Suddenly, energy returns. Hmmm! How does this happen? Our capacity to act into a feeling is restricted *only* by our motivation for doing so.

When you have a compelling reason, you can reach your emotional goals. When your mission is stronger than your mood, you can experience your full potential. You can sit around and wait for those feelings to be triggered from the outside, or you can behave your way into those blessings now. After all, the word *emotion* itself is 86 percent *motion.*

When you behave in a way that's pleasing to God, you will be rewarded with the emotional fruits you desire. And when we enthusiastically follow God's principles even when we don't feel like it, we'll soon experience the joy that comes from pleasing our Creator. It's a definite leap of faith to act in a manner consistent with what you want to feel, but consider the alternative!

ACTIVATE 4:8

Drill #31

As you just read, what we *do* can have a dramatic effect on how we *feel*. In the space below, list three of your emotional goals. Beside each, identify an activity that helps bring about the desired emotion, either directly or indirectly. At the bottom, indicate what aspect of your life could most benefit from your doing the right thing whether you feel like it or not.

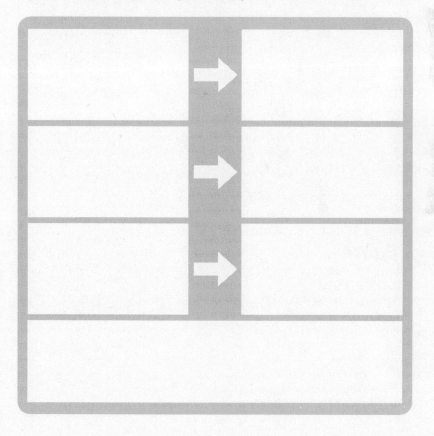

The Extra Mile

Write a brief condensation of today's lesson, summarizing the key points that hit home with you. E-mail this summary to yourself and up to eight friends who you believe will appreciate and benefit from the message.

Make It Stick: Thought of the Day

I take charge of my emotions!

Prayer

Father God, thank you for giving me the courage and discipline to do what you want me to do, whether or not I feel like it. Amen.

YOU ARE GOOD AT CERTAIN STUFF FOR A REASON

The Joy of Using Your Strengths

YOU ARE GOOD at certain stuff for a reason. God made you that way intentionally so you can joyfully accomplish his purpose during your lifetime.

You are also lousy at a bunch of things as well. The lousy list will always be longer than the good list because there are lots of other people in this world who are really good at the things that you are not. If you spend a lot of time on the lousy stuff, you will sacrifice a bunch of joy.

This is a strange way to encourage you, isn't it? Stick with me, though. It is all part of God's plan. Think about it: if you were good at everything, there would be lots of unnecessary people just hanging out, doing nothing, occupying who knows what. Some people pretend to be good at everything, but don't be fooled. They are not. They are, however, very good at pretending, and we should at least give them credit for that. Unknowingly, though, these pretenders water down their own potential doing too many things that God created other people to do.

And since God made us on purpose as relational beings, he wants us to collaborate with each other to accomplish his work. In fact, he's created billions of people to get his job done. I don't know exactly how this works, of course, but I imagine that among the billions, there would have to be a few alternates in case some fail to execute his plan and instead choose to exercise their own plans. My point is that we all have roles to fill and missions to accomplish on the very tight deadlines that are our lifetimes.

If you are still alive, God has plans for you, and his plans blow your plans away. This is not a guess but a fact. If you don't believe me, ask God to give you a glimpse of his plan and then compare it to your plan. See which one you prefer.

I believe God has a particular objective for your life. Do you? This objective, or purpose for your life, coincides with your gifts, talents, passions, and a host of other heavenly factors. Your areas of interest—the activities and pursuits that you find most enjoyable, energizing, and attractive—are the best indicators of strong talent and giftedness.

In school, for example, some people are naturally good at math, while others are naturally good at science or English. Of course, educators want us to be good at everything. Many parents do as well. So if we are really good in English but not so good in math, we are invited to stay after school and work on . . . you guessed it, math. Over time, we get the message that the key to a wonderful life is to fix our weaknesses. As kids, we follow the advice and strive to become less weak at our weaknesses while we simultaneously become weaker at our strengths. Could something possibly be wrong with this picture?

Some people are really good at sports and others at singing or painting. Some people are neat and organized and always color inside the lines. Others have a harder time accepting these boundaries. As adults, some have analytical strengths, while others build great relationships, design amazing marketing campaigns, or deliver moving and memorable sermons.

When you engage in activities that demand your special talent, your brain releases chemicals that trigger within you a sense of satisfaction and significance as an incentive for you to continue in this area. I never experienced this chemical reaction in math. But I did experience this joy with baseball, later with coaching, and subsequently even more so with writing and speaking. This strong and encouraging sense of satisfaction is a positive reinforcement mechanism that is all part of God's perfect design.

Our talents eventually get converted into strengths if we fully engage them and sustain the course long enough. We tend to gain great joy from operating in our area of strength. Consequently, we practice and participate over and over again because it makes us feel so good. With roughly half of our waking hours devoted to our work life, it better bring us great joy! If our work is both our mission and our ministry, it no doubt will.

Our unique conglomeration of character, talents, life experiences, personality, and even struggles merge together and spark a vision within each of us. The more often we engage in our strengths, the more crystallized our ultimate vision becomes and the greater things God can do through us. With our God-given talents transformed into strengths, we become intrinsically motivated, needing less and less prodding from the outside. And this repetitive practice produces champions capable of making giant contributions in the world.

Will you be one of them?

ACTIVATE 4:8

Drill #32

In today's drill, I'll force you to give mental airtime to your top strengths. On the following page, indicate three areas where you shine. Next to each, identify what you could do in the next month to better deploy your strengths in the world. Then, at the bottom, record the first steps you will take to become more conscious of your strengths every day.

The Extra Mile

For two consecutive weeks, track how many of your waking hours you spend doing things that you consider to be personal strengths. Consider this number your starting point. Going forward, make it a priority to increase your "strength time," even if just a little, every single week. Keep a record of recurring distractions and obligations that inhibit your expression of strength so that you can develop a plan to minimize these barriers.

Make It Stick: Thought of the Day

I focus on my strengths!

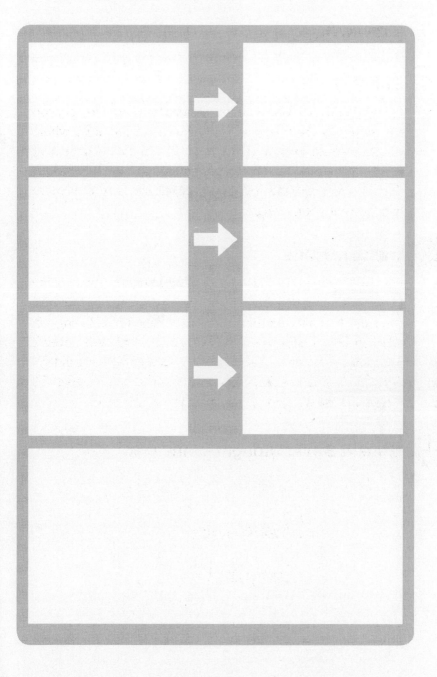

Prayer

Heavenly Father, thank you for matching my special talents with your particular purpose for me. Help me today to elevate my strengths, accept my weaknesses, and collaborate with others to bring glory to you. Amen.

DAY
33

WHAT'S YOUR GOAL?

The Joy of Being His Greatest Creation

AS I MENTIONED way back in day five, humans think in one of two primary ways. The most common is in reaction to the world around us, similar to how an animal in the woods reacts to a noise or a threat. Often we simply respond to whatever someone else does or to an experience we have. We react with a particular thought that, if it persists, generates an emotion, followed by an action consistent with that feeling. *We move from thought to emotion to action.*

If we interpret the situation negatively, the resulting emotion is likely to be self-defeating. The behavior that follows will probably move us away from what we really want, even though it may feel right and defensible at the moment. These emotional reflexes quickly become habits of mind.

The other way we can trigger thoughts is intentionally or proactively. We can create a *"to think" list* like the one Paul provides in Philippians 4:8, or we can simply borrow his. We can decide that lovely, gracious, pure, and excellent thoughts are constructive and the kind we want to think on a regular basis. Deliberately choosing 4:8 Thoughts produces the emotional life we want. They will stimulate good moods, and these moods will spur action consistent with the goals and ideals most important to us.

You can create a *virtuous cycle* like this by getting really clear on your personal vision and aligning your behavior with that vision, thereby producing the emotional blessings you desire. Your vision is the mental picture you hold of your future. If that image is definite, compelling, and detailed, it exerts a powerful influence on your current decisions, pulling you in the direction of your dreams. The alternative is to surrender your emotional life to the events of the day and live in constant suspense, acting consistently with your ideals only when you *feel* like it.

Understand that your emotional strength is directly linked to your moral decisions. The choices you make that violate biblical truth invite emotional discord, even though they may initially produce counterfeit joy. This emotional debt must always be paid back, with interest. But when you behave in ways that are pleasing to God, you will be rewarded with the emotional fruit that your soul truly desires. When you live purposefully, think rightly, serve generously, and forgive quickly, you are laying the groundwork for emotional victory. I have found it very empowering to remind myself repeatedly that negative emotions are not God's will for my life.

Throughout this book, I have offered ample strategies for dealing with negative emotions so that you can move closer to a joy-filled life. As your coach, my goal is to help you reach this goal. But first we have to come to grips with this fundamental question: *If it comes down to choosing between experiencing joy or experiencing the negative emotion you believe you deserve, what's it going to be?*

In other words, as I've said before, "Deal or No Deal?"

We have all been in situations where we've almost enjoyed wallowing in negative emotions. We nurse a grudge against someone who said something hurtful, or we sulk in response to being disappointed. But what is the end result? Will acting on the negative emotion move us in the direction of our highest good? Will that negative emotion bless those closest to us? Will it help us reach our goals? In a marriage spat, for example, is the goal to be right or to be happy?

What's your goal?

I bombard my clients with this question for the purpose of activating their God-given reason and conscience, thereby enhancing their spontaneous decision making. Your goal should act as a filter, eliminating words, behaviors, and other emotional responses that oppose it.

As a parent, for example, your emotional responses can be tempered by a clearly stated parenting goal—such as communicating love, not impatience, to your children—that weeds out irresponsible parental reactions regardless of their apparent justification.

Certainly, you will have negative triggers in your life from time to time. Fortunately, God has provided a little gap of opportunity for his most valuable creation. This tiny space between the stimuli and your response to it gives you a chance to think before you react. This will shape not only your potential for joy but also your destiny as a human being.

What's your goal?

ACTIVATE 4:8 :::::::::::::::::::::::::::::

Drill #33

Identify up to three recurring stressful or difficult situations involving important people in your life. Then describe the goal or positive outcome you would prefer to see for each. Finally, clarify how you intend to respond (in the gap) to preserve your joy and reach your goal.

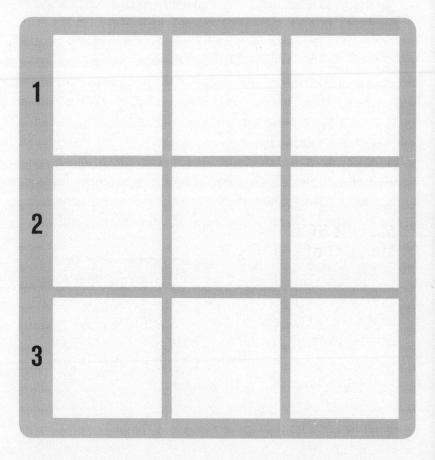

The Extra Mile

Create a list of the specific emotions you would like to experience more often over the upcoming year. Then identify the specific negative emotions you would like to experience less over the coming year. Review this list weekly and begin thinking and speaking in a manner consistent with the emotions you desire.

_____

_____

_____

_____

_____

_____

Make It Stick:
Thought of the Day

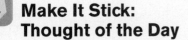

What's my goal?

Prayer

Lord, thank you for the joy that comes from following you. Help me today to deliberately choose words and actions that are lovely, excellent, and worthy of praise—words and actions that will help me meet my goal. Amen.

THE MASTER'S MIND

The Joy of His Thoughts

YOU DON'T NEED any special instruction or coaching to think like most people think. Common thinking is common thinking for the very reason that it follows the path of least resistance. Without an outside influence challenging and equipping us to think differently, we will follow the path of 8:4 Thinking, highlighting the deficiencies that surround us.

Unfortunately, the gravitational pull of human nature on our thinking patterns causes the majority of people to miss out on the joy-filled life. Consider that it takes virtually no effort to be negative, cynical, and pessimistic. This attitudinal black hole just happens naturally. But the power of negativity is immense. It corrodes our faith. It weakens our immunity. It zaps our energy. It compromises our relationships. And, of course, it robs us of the joy our heavenly Father intends for us.

Joy, on the other hand, is a gift from God. However, it does have strings attached—meaning that we have a hand in our own joy and that negativity, in whatever costume it appears, is largely a self-inflicted wound. While the preceding sentence may at first seem to be a bummer, it is exactly the opposite. It is great news for you and for me: we have a choice.

By the grace of God, each moment is a mental sunrise, a new beginning and fresh opportunity to become who he desires for you to be. Your thoughts can become totally different, and as a result, your character can change and your life can be transformed. God wants you to be completely alive, full of passion, and bursting with joy. After all, we're his children—and would you want anything less for your children?

You can become everything God had in mind when he created you. Despite your past and regardless of your current circumstances, your future can exceed even your wildest expectations. There is only one catch: *you must learn to think like God thinks!*

You may be wondering, *How could I possibly do that?* Well, of course it's impossible to literally think like God—he is all-knowing and all-powerful. But we can learn to focus our thoughts on things that reflect his character and agree with his promises.

To understand how God thinks, we must first comprehend who God is. With just a quick glimpse through the Bible, we learn the following truths about who God is:

God is love.
God is all-powerful.
God is ever-present.
God is all-knowing.
God is absolute truth.
God is holy.
God is merciful.

God is faithful.
God is just.
God is unchanging.

Though not exhaustive, this description of God's nature certainly gives us enough clues to contemplate the perfection and unlimited character of our Creator. To think like God, you must become intentional about mirroring his image in all that you do. Nowhere is this more important than in your thought life. Clearly, God's thoughts are substantive and consequential. The more you dwell on and with God, the more valuable and less trivial your thinking becomes. Paul writes, "Let this mind be in you which was also in Christ Jesus" (Philippians 2:5, NKJV). Ask yourself, *What would Jesus think?*

In Jeremiah 17:9, we are reminded that the human heart is "deceitful above all things" (NKJV). Therefore, we desperately need God's help. Admit your dependence on him and ask him to transform your heart, which influences your thinking. Then strive to make your thinking as close to God's thinking as possible. Discover God's mind by studying God's Word and pondering his nature. When you worship any characteristic of God, that trait will begin to mature in your own heart. The attributes of God always grow in the heart that appreciates them.

As perplexing and unhip as it may be to the rest of the world, as a Christian you can think like God thinks because you have the mind of Christ (1 Corinthians 2:16). When your thinking disagrees with his, reclaim the truth and "take captive every thought to make it obedient to Christ" (2 Corinthians 10:5, NIV). It's not easy, but it is simpler than you might realize—and it will pay great dividends. The truly difficult thing is living with the consequences of *not* changing the way you think.

God wants to impart his character and power through every individual. And when this happens, the world is instantly changed because those who reflect his glory impact the world. As you know by now, the Scripture verse on which this book is based is Philippians 4:8, written by the apostle Paul:

> Whatever things are true, whatever things are noble, whatever things are just, whatever things are pure, whatever things are lovely, whatever things are of good report, if there is any virtue and if there is anything praiseworthy—meditate on these things. (NKJV)

This verse reflects crisply the very nature and character of God, who himself is true, noble, just, pure, lovely, and of good report. As Christians, we are called to meditate on things that mirror God's character! Not only does this keep us from focusing on sinful or destructive things, but it also allows us to fill our lives with hope and optimism.

ACTIVATE 4:8

Drill #34

Today's drill is a bit of an accountability checkup. Reflect back on the last month as you have been working through this forty-day program, and confess to yourself on the following page the things that you have thought, said, or done that do not reflect 4:8 Thinking. Then indicate how you would handle those situations if you had another chance. Finally, at the bottom, jot down any additional ideas for improvement.

The Extra Mile

Reread today's lesson and do a little research in your Bible on the mind of Christ. Then pick one area of life (career, marriage, etc.) and, for just one day, concentrate all your mental attention

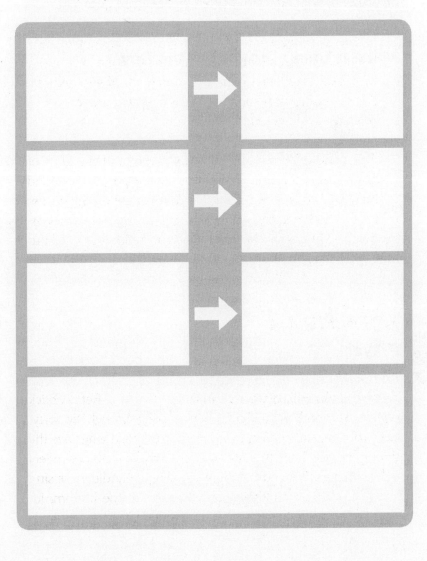

on thinking like God thinks. All day long, be extra mindful of where your thoughts are taking you. Ask the question, What would Jesus think? If you sense you are drifting away from his thoughts, gently pull yourself back in the right direction. Focus on progress, not perfection. Repeat this exercise once a month.

Make It Stick: Thought of the Day

> I am learning to think like God thinks!

Prayer

Lord, thank you for the peace, joy, and power of your thinking. Help me to think like you do. Amen.

GOD WILL BE CHEERING!

The Joy of Discovery

WHAT ARE YOUR Christmas mornings like? As far back as I can remember, there's been a crowd at mine. I can't remember a Christmas that didn't involve at least nine family members. The list included my parents, a couple of grandmothers, four sisters, and me. As the years passed, the group size has multiplied more than three times. It's funny how that works. Even with the loss of grandparents, the Christmas celebration at my parents' home recently reached an all-time high with thirty family members. This included my wife and our three sons, my parents, my four sisters, their husbands, my fourteen nieces and nephews, and my oldest niece's fiancé. We have been blessed indeed. It is always loud, a lot of fun, and over way too quickly.

With such a big crowd, we've learned a few tricks over the years to make the get-togethers run more smoothly. One practice in particular came in very handy when all the grandchildren were small. Imagine twenty-plus people in a room, all opening gifts at the same time. In an attempt to minimize the mess, we started passing out large plastic trash bags before we opened gifts. Each family had a bag (or two or three) and was encouraged to clean up as they opened packages, stuffing the wrapping paper, bows, ribbons, and boxes into the trash bags to avoid a massive cleanup at the end. At least that was the plan.

Inevitably, though, the efficiency didn't always translate into effectiveness. On several occasions, an overeager family member or two (names withheld) inadvertently disposed of something essential. Instead of just getting rid of the mess, they got rid of the gift itself. And the tinier the present, the greater the chance that it might get scooped up and trapped in one of the garbage bags soon to be hauled out of the house and out of sight. Fast forward a few hours . . .

"Has anyone seen an earring lying around?"

"Did anybody see an envelope with a gift certificate inside?"

"Where are the batteries to my fire truck?"

"I can't find the charger for my new phone."

"I'm missing a . . ."

Of course, nobody had seen anything. There were no witnesses. Everyone knew what this meant, and it was not good news. If no one had seen it and it didn't walk away, it had to be in one of those ten or so trash bags back behind the house.

By this time in the afternoon, those bags weren't just filled with discarded wrapping paper. They now contained the collateral damage of a holiday feast. So if we were serious about finding what we lost, we would have to pick a bag and start digging. The remnants of Christmas dinner, a not-so-fresh diaper, signs that someone may have had a bad cold, and who knows what else were the obstacles that stood between us and our objective.

If we wanted to recover the missing gift, we would have to pay the price and dig through the muck. So we held our noses, put on gloves, and searched the trash like CSI detectives hunting for evidence. If we were determined, we usually found what we were looking for. The celebratory "I found it" scream could be heard all over the house. The jewelry had been found. The gift certificate had been recovered.

As a life coach for over two decades, I have developed a conviction that reminds me of the family Christmases I just described. I believe that God made each of us for a particular purpose, and until we discover this true place, part of our joy will be hidden from us and certain things will never seem quite right.

Too often, we get so busy dealing with lots of stuff (the wrappings and trappings) in our busy lives that it becomes easy to lose what really matters. Until the noise and chatter dies down a bit, we may not even notice it is missing.

But once we realize that we've lost something meaningful, we naturally want to go find it. And we should be willing to do whatever it takes to make the recovery. We each have a calling, a divinely infused mission that will serve others and bring great joy at the same time. If you've lost this sense of direction, go look for it.

As I wrote in my book *Success Is Not an Accident*, "I believe that God's will for you is something wonderful and glorious—far better than anything you could ever sit down and design for yourself."[6] Nothing quite supercharges your potential for joy like living in sync with God's purpose for your life. Moreover, God experiences great joy when you follow the path he has etched on your heart. Some of us are passionately seeking this purpose. Others are trying to find what we lost. Many haven't even recognized yet that our gifts are missing.

Without a deep sense of purpose, life is devoid of true significance or long-term meaning. This type of existence is characterized by going through the motions, cynicism, pessimism, apathy, and ultimately a life of mediocrity. It is perpetual survival mode. It's a life that constantly needs to be filled up with things from the outside—with busyness, distractions, and continuous activity.

You have no greater responsibility than to determine what God put you here on earth to accomplish. Ask him to help you find it. Refuse to let yourself die a common copy. Don't conform to the average life. Be an original. Accept that you have been custom made by God to serve an exclusive function in this world, even if that role and a plan to fulfill it are not yet clear to you. This is your true place—and it's up to you to find it, no matter how difficult it may be.

There are no extra human beings. Your true place is your unique path to glorifying God. When you arrive in your true place, you will know it. A sense of destiny will come over you as what you most love to do merges with what you do best. This is where you will be investing your life in *God's* way, making the difference that only you are uniquely equipped to make. While each of us has many different paths where we could do well in life, there is but one particular thing that God had in mind when he made you. For some, this true place will shake the entire world. For others, it will soothe just one tiny home. In either case, the world will be left a better place.

The more you experience your true place, the more you will be drawn to it. The nagging hint of dissatisfaction, which maybe only you knew existed, will disappear. You will enjoy invigorating surges of self-worth, as there will no longer be a need to compare yourself with anyone else. You will be healthier, more prosperous, and full of joy.

What is God whispering in your ear? It takes courage, not conformity, to honestly identify where you have been uniquely blessed—where you have special talents and abilities. No matter how far you may have strayed from your purpose, you can always find it again. Your true place is always waiting for you because no one but you can fill it. Meditate on that thought!

Take comfort in knowing that every experience you have ever had, no matter how seemingly unrelated, can be used to your advantage in your true place when you finally find it. And you will find it . . . if you will wholeheartedly look for it.

The dream God plants in your heart, in your DNA, will not come to fruition by accident. All along the path, you will face resistance—institutional, cultural, relational, financial, and mental. This is simply part of the game.

You must press on in the face of all the pressure to conform. You must take action that leaves no doubt you are committed to your ultimate vision—and you must do this before you have the money, before you have the confidence, and even before you have the blessing of those closest to you.

Now more than ever, the world needs people like you to use their God-given talents to make a positive difference. You may have to sift through some clutter and other junk to find what you've lost, but be encouraged: you will find it if you start looking.

And when you find this true place, you can surely celebrate. God will be cheering for you!

ACTIVATE 4:8 :::::::::::::::::::::::::::::::

Drill #35

Are you purposefully moving toward your true place? Today's drill prompts you to examine where you are right now. In the first column on the following page, identify up to three examples that suggest you may not be where you need to be. In the second column, identify any evidence that suggests you are already on track. In the third column, devise three action steps that would likely move you closer to your true place.

The Extra Mile

Persistently ask God these three questions: Who am I? Why am I here? Where do you want me to go? Ask God to reveal his will for you through your desires.

Make It Stick: Thought of the Day

I have found my true place!

AREAS FOR GROWTH	ON TRACK	ACTION

Prayer

Heavenly Father, thank you for making me deliberately. Reveal to me today what I need to know to live on purpose and in my true place, arranged just for me. Amen.

OWN, STARVE, RETREAT

The Joy of Solutions

AS I'VE SAID BEFORE, I generally find more value in looking forward than in looking back. So in today's lesson, I will not prompt you to unearth the past or resolve issues from your childhood. Instead, I am going to equip you with three additional approaches for dealing with your emotions *today* so that you can reap more joy *tomorrow*.

My clients have found these recommendations to be beneficial and remarkably simple to implement. Since your objective is to make the joy-filled life your emotional set point, incorporate the ideas that most appeal to you or are most relevant to your situation at the moment.

Remember, most people wing it through life, never really considering what they are thinking about or the consequences of those thoughts. Most of our friends, family, and coworkers react impulsively to the world around them. But it doesn't have to be this way. I'm confident that if you put these strategies into place, you'll become more skilled at dealing with your emotions in a way that will multiply your joy.

First, *own your negative emotions*. This means accepting responsibility for the thoughts that have redirected your emotions in a southerly direction. Sure, you can justify all day long why you deserve to be upset, but what do you gain from that kind of mind-set? If your intention is to live with maximum joy, then own your reactions by boldly (or silently) declaring, "I am responsible." Initially, you don't even have to believe this completely. Affirming that you're responsible for your own reactions, even if you have to grit your teeth to do it, deflates negative emotions via the Law of Exchange. (Remember, you can do away with a negative thought only by replacing it with a positive thought.)

The three words *I am responsible* withhold the emotional oxygen blame needs to survive. The moment you stop blaming others, you're on the road to greater emotional health. The common tendency in our society is to blame people or events for causing us to feel and act the way we do. Whenever you catch yourself going down that tired path, activate the Law of Exchange and say to yourself, *I am responsible*. The first few times you say it, it may not feel genuine. Continue to repeat it, because you know that it is the truth.

No worries—you're not accepting legal liability for negative situations. You are not proclaiming that another person didn't contribute to the problem. What you are doing is refusing to be brought down to a lower level because of what someone else does. Do not let another person determine your frame of mind; life is too short for that. Even if you can't stomach accepting any responsibility for the situation you find yourself in, you are still responsible for what you do about it. You are responsible for your reaction and whether it improves or worsens your circumstances.

The next time you start to feel negative, repeat those gut-wrenching words: *I am responsible.* Say them to yourself. Say them aloud, if possible. Very quickly, those negative, joy-suppressing thoughts will not feel welcome in your mental house. They will go and find somebody else who will coddle them.

Starving negative emotions is another amazingly effective approach for preserving your joy. In the midst of a negative episode, when you are feeling angry or discouraged or hurt, tune in to the big picture. Step back a bit and remind yourself of what's truly important. A change in perspective can interrupt negative momentum and activate your reason, allowing you to quickly reframe the heat in the moment. When you stop feeding your negative emotions, they will begin to fade.

If I had the opportunity to coach you in the middle of a difficult emotional period, I would ask you these questions:

- What is your goal here?
- What outcome do you want in this situation?
- What's your vision?
- Will the negative state that you're in move you toward your goal, or will it move you in another direction?

Then I would have you ask yourself these questions:

- Where is this situation headed, and is that okay?
- What do I really want?
- What's most important here?
- How might my negativity affect this relationship?

- Is my integrity at stake here?
- Could my health be more important than proving my point right now?

When you give up the need to be right, you expand your options and experience joy instead of distress. Only after seeing the big picture can you fully grasp that the negative situation you saw before was only a small part of the whole. From a different vantage point, difficulties can appear quite different in size, scope, and solvability. Thinking beyond the current moment eliminates tunnel vision and promotes wise and measured responses. When you put your problem in perspective, you starve the negative emotions that too often feed on your anxiety.

Finally, *temporarily retreating from your issues* can be an effective approach for reclaiming your equilibrium and retaining your joy. No, this doesn't mean I am giving you permission to run away from your problems. But sometimes when you are in a down emotional state, the cause is a complete mystery. You may not be able to pinpoint anything that is specifically bothering you. In other cases, the trigger is quite obvious. Becoming adept at quickly recognizing your low moods is a skill worth developing. If you are unaware of your negative frame of mind, then the thoughts, words, and actions that follow can quickly fuel a negative spiral, and recovery will consume significant time, energy, and goodwill.

In these situations, it is wise to consider the option of temporary retreat. Staying in the presence of others might inadvertently fuel your fire. Briefly withdrawing, especially from loved ones, allows the time-tested wisdom of "this too shall pass" to kick in and start working to your advantage. Reminding yourself of this truth supplies a vision of closure and weakens the grip of negative emotions. It gives you something to hope for and an opportunity to practice your faith.

From time to time, you may find it therapeutic to back away, shut the door, be alone, and allow the fire of negative emotions to die down of its own accord. As children, most of us experienced this dynamic when we were sent to our rooms for a little while to cool off and "sober up" emotionally. Unless you're still living with your parents, you may have forgotten how well this works.

Though retreating may not resolve the situation, it limits the damage by protecting you from yourself. When you're feeling really negative, it is like being emotionally inebriated. The information transmitted from your brain is skewed to some degree in these circumstances, and trusting this faulty feedback will lead only to poor decisions that make life worse. Keep the faith and your composure as well. As the negative clouds pass—and they will—solutions will seem much more apparent.

Remember these three strategies—own your negative emotions, starve those negative emotions, and when prudent, temporarily retreat—and experience more joy.

ACTIVATE 4:8

Drill #36

Consider a current difficulty or chronic unpleasant circumstance you are facing. On the following page, note three ways that you could accept responsibility for where things are today.

The Extra Mile

Identify an important individual (maybe your child) or group of individuals (maybe a Sunday school class) and offer to teach today's lesson on emotional control. Prepare your lesson outline, incorporating relevant examples from your life as well as those ideas you deem worthwhile from the rest of this book. Then present the lesson in your own words and in your own style.

Make It Stick: Thought of the Day

> I am responsible for how I think.

Prayer

Heavenly Father, thanks for the lifelong challenge of managing my emotions. Enable me today to see the big picture and respond to difficult people and demanding situations with wisdom and grace. Amen.

THE MENTALIST

The Joy of Focus

WE THINK. We feel. We act. We become.

Because of our thinking, we feel certain emotions. As a result of these feelings, we engage in certain behaviors. And these behaviors accumulate and produce the conditions of our lives. We are, in fact, "the mentalist" of our own existence, not because we have superior powers of some sort, but because we have the *simple* power to choose what we think about all day long.

In the CBS television series *The Mentalist,* the main character, Patrick Jane, uses his supposed mental powers as a former psychic medium to help investigators solve cases. Ironically, Jane's previous career as a medium was nothing but a ruse, as Jane doesn't even believe people have psychic abilities. Nonetheless, he leveraged his own mental capacity by understanding human nature and teaching himself to be a keen observer and shrewd analytic when assisting in criminal investigations. Like this fictional character, we don't need special powers; we just need to make good use of what we already have.

Since so few elect to use this mental power, it comes across as quite special when it is employed. Although you cannot create your world directly, or even create your feelings directly, you do so indirectly by the way in which you choose to think. To varying degrees, you bring about what you think about. Your thinking makes your life experience junky or joyous, depending on the handpicked thoughts you entertain most consistently.

Mental discipline is the learned skill of keeping your mind centered on productive thoughts, even when turbulent, distracting thoughts are swirling in your vicinity. This requires continuous upward progress. And as you know by now, mental discipline precedes emotional discipline. With high levels of mental discipline, you reach your goals faster, experience more joy, and become a lot more fun to be around. Virtually any meaningful goal is within reach when you become mentally disciplined.

Without mental discipline, even relatively easy goals become a strain. With weak mental muscles, your emotional life is arbitrary and unpredictable. Mental laziness slowly dissolves your potential for greatness—first internally and then outwardly.

By deliberately working to improve your mental game, you will upgrade every area of your life. You will hit your business objectives faster. Your family life will be more peaceful. With strong, toned mental muscles, you'll be more fit spiritually, emotionally, and physically.

This exceptional mental focus involves four components, all of which can be intentionally cultivated. The first is *clarity* about what is to be accomplished, both in the immediate moment and the long term. Without a precise target to shoot for, your thought life will bounce back and forth between competing objectives and non-objectives. It's critical to know both what needs to be accomplished right now, such as with writing a business proposal or improving a golf swing, and what needs to be accomplished in the long-term, such as increasing annual revenue or reaching a certain golf handicap. When your "now goals" are in alignment with your "then goals," you are primed for mental discipline.

The next component is *concentration*, referring to how well you stay engaged in the current moment and fixed on what's important now. One of my coaches used to call this the "how in the now." Anything less than 100 percent concentration reveals divided attention and double-mindedness. Distractions are simply misplaced attractions that downgrade your potential. Surprisingly, multitasking is the nastiest villain when it comes to interrupting pure concentration. Another common trap includes physically being at home, but mentally being at the office. Often distractions arise from "losing the moment" by dwelling on an unchangeable past experience or worrying about a future situation. Build up your concentration.

Confidence is your belief in your capability to reach a particular goal. While genuine confidence is rooted in actual accomplishment, past performance alone does not ensure that you'll develop or maintain confidence. Sustainable self-confidence grows from exhaustive preparation, winning moments, positive memories, and a focus on incremental progress instead of perfection. To build positive memories, dwell on and record your best accomplishments from week to week. In other words, "Think 4:8!"

Finally, *challenge* refers to the degree of demand that you willingly place on yourself. Your mental discipline will rise to meet the goal that you establish. Small goals extract only surface potential, while huge goals release untapped reserves and trigger unforeseen breakthroughs. Most people just want the easy button. They think in terms of minimum or "good enough." They use their energy to evade the pressure moments and spotlight situations that introduce champions to the world. Ironically, your best self is revealed when the stakes are high, when the deadline is looming, and when the game is on the line.

Seek opportunities that require loads of mental discipline, and you'll be surprised at the treasure you find. Anyone can occasionally experience peak performance; we can all have a great day now and then. Your standard, though, is much higher. Like a world-class athlete, when you master mental discipline, you will find yourself replicating your best performance at will.

When you do, you will find you have what it takes not only to hit your life goals even faster, but also to become a world-class human being in the process. And what a joy that will be!

ACTIVATE 4:8 :::::::::::::::::::::::::::

Drill #37

For today's drill, consider the overall condition of your life right now. Then make two short lists. On List One, write three things (anything) you want to minimize in your life. On List Two, write three things (anything) you want to increase in your life. Emphasize List Two by coloring it with a bright highlighter.

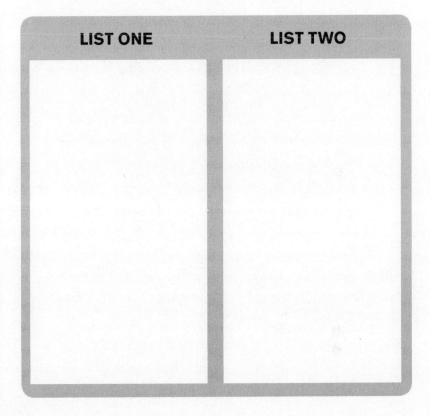

The Extra Mile

For the next six weeks, either by hand or digitally, capture and record your daily progress toward your goals, including achievements, improvements, positive experiences, "aha moments," and compliments received. Review early and often.

Make It Stick: Thought of the Day

> I am clear, focused, & mentally disciplined!

Prayer

Father, thank you for the potency of my thought life. For today, please steer my thinking so that I bring out the best in myself and the important people in my life. Amen.

ROUTINE OR EXCEPTIONAL

The Joy of Thanksgiving

ROUTINE GRATITUDE is standard gratitude. It is ordinary, reactive, and often superficial. This includes saying thank you after receiving a gift or being helped. For example, when someone lets you in as you're merging into traffic, you wave a thank-you to the other driver. When somebody holds a door for you, you smile and say thank you. When you're handed your food in the drive-through window, you thank the server. These are all typical instances of *routine gratitude*.

Some people develop an immediate sense of gratefulness and relief when they hear about an accident or a tragedy in someone else's life. This rocks them out of their complacency, and they feel grateful for their own life and safety as a result. This is also routine gratitude. Wouldn't it be wonderful, though, if we didn't need other people's sorrows to remind us of the blessings in our own lives?

In today's world, it is easy to become desensitized to all but the most horrendous tragedies. We can overhear somebody talking about a horrible car crash or a crime that was committed, and it blows right over our heads. It just skims the surface; it hardly even bothers us. It even appears that the reactive yet intense gratitude for our freedom, our families, and our faith triggered by the events of September 11, 2001, has already been dulled by the passage of time, at least for those without loved ones directly involved. Routine gratitude feels sincere at the time, but it hasn't penetrated the heart.

The good news is that you have the option of moving to a whole new level of appreciation and thanksgiving. I call it *exceptional gratitude.*

Exceptional gratitude is intentional, proactive, extraordinary, and consistent with the 4:8 Principle. Anyone can be appreciative of something obvious, but it takes a joy-filled person to perceive the mustard seed of potential in a thorny situation or a difficult individual. Expressing thanks for even the smallest things is where routine gratitude ends and exceptional gratitude starts.

Exceptional gratitude refers to acts of thankfulness unprompted by someone else's tragedy, pain, or misfortune. Exceptional gratitude doesn't require something to be missing before it's appreciated. This kind of gratitude is what Paul had in mind when he wrote to the Thessalonians, "Give thanks in all circumstances; for this is God's will for you in Christ Jesus" (1 Thessalonians 5:18, NIV).

Sadly, we often act as if we're going to live forever, as if today is merely a dress rehearsal. We think we can always show up, catch up, or make up tomorrow. We convince ourselves that we'll get another chance—but life doesn't always work out that way. Have you ever wondered if the victim of today's car crash remembered to tell her family how much she loved them? Was she aware of how much they really appreciated her?

Every morning, unsuspecting people all over the world walk out their front door never to return home, victims of accidents, heart attacks, violence, and other unpredictable instances of sudden death. When you practice exceptional gratitude, you enjoy the peace of knowing that you've said what needs to be said and that you've appreciated the most important people in your life.

Exceptional gratitude also means staying aware of universal blessings, the things that benefit everyone. It involves experiencing the power of gratitude through those things that are common to us all:

- God's love
- our bodies
- our brains
- sunshine and rain
- forests and deserts
- mountains and beaches
- freedom in all forms
- technology
- relationships
- and much more . . .

Exceptional gratitude means expressing thankfulness for the little things in life that aren't so little, such as smiles, hugs, music, indoor plumbing, air-conditioning, clean water, science, education, seat belts, antibiotics, our immune system, and second chances, just to scratch the surface.

Exceptional gratitude also involves making a habit of appreciating other people. When something appreciates, it increases in value, right? When people are sincerely appreciated, their own self-worth is elevated as well. If you want to increase the value of something in your life, take better care of it. If you want to increase the value of key relationships, treasure them.

Perhaps your spouse could really benefit from some exceptional gratitude. Or possibly it is your child or even your parents who are starving for appreciation. Maybe it is a key coworker or a priority client. Whoever they are, take better care of them. Honor them with more interest and attention. Dwell on what's good about them—there is always something that's great or could be great. View them through the lens of Philippians 4:8. And there is a special bonus when you appreciate others: it increases not only their value but yours as well.

On more than one occasion, I have received a note, a phone call, or an e-mail at just the right time that inspired me to go another mile—to study more, write more, speak more, encourage more, and strive to be more than I would have been otherwise. I've been the recipient of exceptional gratitude.

How about you? Does your gratitude stand out above the crowd? Remember, by giving more gratitude, you get to keep more joy.

ACTIVATE 4:8 ::::::::::::::::::::::::::::::::

Drill #38

Fast forward five years or more and pinpoint a specific date. Contemplate the future blessings that you hope to be experiencing at that point, and write up to eight of them on the following page.

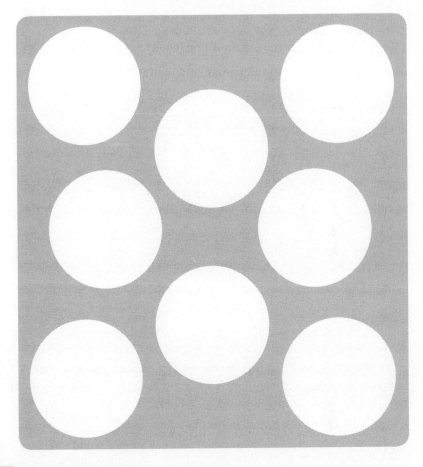

The Extra Mile

Select one person—friend, family member, or coworker—who has helped you in some way in the last week, and send a quick text of gratitude. Next, identify one person who has been a special blessing to you in the last year, and send him or her a brief thank-you e-mail. Finally, think of an individual from the past who was particularly supportive and encouraging, and handwrite a note of appreciation. Mail it today.

Make It Stick: Thought of the Day

I am actively grateful for my blessings.

Prayer

Lord, thank you for covering me with your goodness. Help me today to notice and actively appreciate the big and little blessings that surround me. Amen.

DAY
39

CUT THE CLUTTER

The Joy of Simplicity

NO PLAN FOR THE JOY-FILLED LIFE can be complete without a proposal to cut the clutter. Clutter breeds discontent, while simplicity breeds joy. Clutter smothers joy, while simplicity liberates it. Clutter makes life complicated, heavy, and wearisome. Simplicity makes life relaxed, carefree, and invigorating.

In today's lesson, I'll challenge you to develop your own blueprint for minimizing clutter so you can continue maximizing joy. To help you better understand the nature of clutter, let me share a very functional definition I use with my clients: clutter is anything that takes up your time and attention but doesn't boost your joy.

Restated, clutter refers to the assortment of things, thoughts, and attitudes that inhibit us from living the life that God meant for us to live. Clutter is the stuff that interferes with our joy. It builds up as a result of normal, everyday activities, just like plaque on our teeth. With proper care, though, we can minimize tooth decay—and with proper care and attention, we can also minimize clutter and the lifestyle decay it causes.

Clutter snatches away our attention from what really matters and transfers it to what barely matters. For all practical purposes, clutter transforms our mind into a junkyard. Instead of having our attention focused on our blessings and passions, it gets redirected toward lingering problems. Clearly, clutter makes it more challenging to focus on what is lovely, pure, true, and excellent.

Vivid one-word descriptions of clutter I share in my workshops include the following:

- stagnation
- congestion
- complexity
- junk
- messes
- incompletion
- stuff
- drain
- negativity
- procrastination
- distraction
- overcommitment
- indecision
- limbo

What words or images are evoked in your mind when you review this list?

Clutter often develops much like the mess created after cooking a gourmet meal. You make a delicious meal, but you also dirty a lot of dishes. No big deal, right? Just clean up the mess. But what happens if you don't clean it up, and instead immediately launch into meal number two? You'll have to work around all the stuff left behind from the first meal.

What happens if you get to meal number four or five and you still haven't cleaned up the original mess? Maybe the pan you need is dirty or the particular spatula or knife you prefer cannot be located. Possibly you have to work on a different side of the kitchen that is poorly lit because there is no room on the main counter. It's not tragic, of course, but at this point, it is bound to negatively influence the quality of your meal and likely the overall enjoyment you experience while cooking.

This dynamic presents itself in people's lives as well. They allow junk to pile up and become overwhelming, causing them to postpone the cleanup even further. They reach a goal (they cooked a great meal), but they never invest the time to clean up the messes that are made along the way. Consequently, they end up having to improvise and work around the hazards created from the accumulating messes.

The good news is this: as soon as you clean up a mess, that misallocated attention can be reclaimed for creative, growth-generating opportunities and purposes. Dealing with the clutter in your life releases an enormous amount of joyful energy.

For greater understanding, it is helpful to subdivide clutter into several categories, but be aware that clutter seldom remains in its own little world.

Spiritual clutter refers to a deficiency of inner peace, often originating from a lack of intimacy with your Creator. In other words, something is interfering with your connection to God.

Emotional clutter includes lack of forgiveness and any other recurring negative feelings such as frustration, fatigue, boredom, resentment, fear, or worry that have not been productively addressed.

Mental clutter refers to misplaced priorities, important things that have been postponed, the inability to stay focused, or areas where you may be emphasizing image management instead of character management.

Physical clutter refers to the disorganization in your surroundings. There is nothing inherently wrong with having cluttered surroundings. What matters is whether your physical environment supports your capability to enjoy life to the fullest or whether it gets in the way. Today's modern lifestyle seems to feed the impulse to hoard. Just consider the recent boom in storage facilities. But have you ever spotted a hearse pulling a U-Haul? PODS aren't parked in cemeteries for a reason.

Financial clutter refers to the messes in your personal economy and could include debt, a weak or nonexistent financial plan, the absence of a budget, insufficient insurance protection, or failing to synchronize with your spouse about money matters.

Legal clutter may include taking the time required to adequately address legal vulnerability, ignoring the task of prudent legal planning, defending against lawsuits, as well as not updating wills and other necessary legal documents.

Relational clutter is often the most emotionally charged and refers to lingering negative emotions toward someone important in your life or unfinished relationship business that is robbing your attention from forward-looking goals.

To better understand the effect that clutter has on your mind-set, think of your mind like your laptop. If you have too many programs running at the same time, your computer's memory may get maxed out. The first symptom may be programs running slowly. The next symptom may be your computer freezing up. Finally, the entire computer may crash. If the computer exhausts its random access memory (RAM), you'll experience even more setbacks and delays.

As human beings, we do not have RAM, but we do function similarly to computers when it comes to allocating our available attention. Instead of RAM, we have, at least conceptually, what I simply call Attention Units (AUs). Like your computer, we do not have an infinite number of these AUs; therefore, we need to be judicious when we deploy them.

Clutter hijacks our mind share, shortchanging the percentage of our attention that is available for positive endeavors such as fellowshiping with God, enjoying relationships, setting goals, solving problems, innovating, and thinking ahead. Your attention units get misallocated, leaving you scattered, smothered, and covered in stuff that pulls you away from what is the highest and wisest use of your time.

Troubled relationships, broken commitments, unwelcome obligations, worry about sick loved ones, financial disorganization, and messy surroundings reflect different types of clutter. But to greater or lesser degrees, all serve as distractions that rob us of AUs that could otherwise be used for productive aims.

Some clutter is inevitable. It just comes with the territory of being human and, especially, being productive. The issue is not so much the clutter itself, but whether we have a system for effectively managing it. One contributing factor in particular seems to spawn additional clutter and complexity: *lack of clarity*. With no clear sense of direction for our lives, we are apt to make a series of fickle decisions, saying yes to the wrong things and no to the right things. We are likely to overextend and overspend, creating a mental tug-of-war and the emotional baggage that accompanies it.

The solution is to correct your vision ahead of time. Make the up-front effort to develop exceptional clarity about your priorities and goals so that it becomes obvious how you should invest your time and money. Bear in mind that clutter universally expands in connection to unwise decisions and broken promises. To avoid getting entangled in onerous commitments that you will later regret, establish the "24-Hour Rule," waiting at least one full day before committing to anything new. During this time, pray, reflect, and assess whether the prospective commitment fits into your mission and long-term goals.

Here are some questions to help you pinpoint the clutter in your life:

- What material possessions have I not used in twenty-four months?
- What is the most important thing I have procrastinated doing?
- What existing obligation or commitment would I not make if I had a do-over?
- What are the chronically stalled projects in my life?
- What current things in my life burn the most energy but return the least reward?
- What activities pull me away from what I most love to do?
- What single action would most increase my peace of mind?

There are two ways to approach busting clutter, and either approach will help you regain the simplicity that is in harmony with joy-filled living. The first is called the chip-away method.

With this approach, you do a little decluttering every day, either until the job is complete or indefinitely as a proactive way to keep all variations of clutter under wraps. I recommend scheduling increments of nine to fourteen minutes per day for this purpose. It doesn't seem like a lot of time, but it adds up fast and you barely feel the impact on your day.

The second approach is called the blitz method. Here you set aside a large chunk of time, such as a twelve- to fourteen-hour day, for the sole purpose of beginning and finishing a single clutter project in one uninterrupted period. This approach suits some personalities really well and is great for handling physical junk projects as well as monotonous financial or legal messes.

Initially, the notion of decluttering your life may not excite you, but if you dwell on the positive feeling you will experience once you're done (4:8 Thinking), you almost instantly become reenergized. When you focus on serving and giving, rather than getting and hoarding, you eliminate spiritual congestion and experience freedom from complexity.

ACTIVATE 4:8

Drill #39

For today's drill, isolate some of the clutter that may be subduing your joy. In the first column on the following page, identify three current clutter projects. Then, to the right, indicate the type of clutter (relational, physical, financial, etc.) and the first step you can take to tackle it once and for all.

CLUTTER	TYPE	FIRST STEP

The Extra Mile

Formulate your own definition of clutter. This goes a long way in controlling it. Then carve out ongoing chunks of time in your calendar each month to take action on both the expected and unexpected clutter that will inevitably surface as you go through life. Schedule this time today!

Make It Stick: Thought of the Day

> I think right
> and travel
> light.

Prayer

Heavenly Father, thank you for the joy of simplicity. Today, show me how to live simply, love deeply, and experience your presence intensely. Amen.

OCCUPY GOD STREET

The Joy of His Presence

GOD'S PRESENCE is everything good.

The joy of his presence is unmatched and unmistakable. His presence amplifies our blessings. It is comforting, purifying, invigorating, inspiring, encouraging, fortifying, and serene all at the same time. It is impossible to experience his presence and remain unchanged.

His presence points us to true north, distinguishing truth from fiction and highlighting significance in an ocean of insignificance. As Psalm 16:11 says, "You make known to me the path of life; you will fill me with joy in your presence, with eternal pleasures at your right hand" (NIV).

His presence shows us where to fully engage and where to rapidly disengage. From the goals we pursue, to how we use our spare moments, to the moral boundaries we establish, his presence shows us when to say yes and when to say no. In his presence our vision is corrected, and we see clearly both the truth and the deception in the world around us.

When we live in his presence, we maximize our present. While God is everywhere, we don't necessarily experience his presence unless we reach out to him and acknowledge him with our thoughts. After all, how else could we experience God's presence except through our thought life? It is always interference on our end, not his, that interrupts this communion with him. When we think selfish, base, impure, and untrue thoughts, we sever the connection and lose the sense of presence that could and should be ours.

In this, the last day of this forty-day boot camp for joy, I want to share with you the single most influential habit you can develop to sustain joy. It is consistent with everything else we have considered, promoted, and practiced during the previous thirty-nine days. *This habit is the intentional cultivation of God's presence.* For refreshing the soul, nothing comes close to steeping in God's presence on a continuous basis. But for most of us, this requires practice.

Today's lesson is about our side of this irreplaceable relationship with our Creator. God handles his side of the relationship perfectly, of course, so our focus will be on ourselves—on the things we can do to amplify his presence inside our own mind.

When we get preoccupied with the problems and pressures of the day, we feel as if we have lost our connection to the ultimate source of our joy and peace. How can we believe in the one true, omnipresent God and yet not experience his presence? What goes wrong? Does he abandon us? If he is always with us, how do we lose the sense of his presence? More important, how do we regain it once it is lost?

Just as we can be living in the same house as our spouse but not experience the closeness that causes the relationship to flourish, God can be with us without us experiencing closeness with him. Living in God's presence requires practice, and with that practice comes the opportunity to have a positively mind-altering experience.

How do we sustain our sense of God's presence in the midst of the trials, trivia, troubles, and tribulations of daily living? When our minds are preoccupied with minor things, we may not be aware of him and the major things he wants us to notice. We must drop those habits of mind and mouth that block his presence. Practicing the presence of God right where we are today allows us to reach a point where we reflexively acknowledge him on a continual basis.

While there are many ways to practice God's presence, here are four practical options that work really well. Each is worthy as a stand-alone approach, but used in conjunction with one another, they can renovate your thought life and prepare your soul for God's occupation.

Appreciate. Go on a gratitude spree. Set the timer on your phone or in your kitchen for four minutes. Then pour out your blessings, big and small. For the greatest impact, record them as you think them. You could record your voice for later playback, or transcribe your blessings into a Word document or a handwritten journal. Do this daily and emphasize the different pieces of your life (past, present, and future) that you are thankful for.

Get into the details. Don't just thank God for your family; thank him for each individual family member and the qualities and experiences you have most appreciated up to this point. Thank God for more than just your health; thank him for each aspect of your body that is functioning properly right now. From day to day, approach this healthy ritual from a fresh perspective. See how many different angles or areas of emphasis you can highlight with this exercise. If you prefer, execute this gratitude spree while exercising, in the shower, or maybe on your drive to work. When you remain consciously aware of your blessings, you stay constantly open to God.

Contemplate. Dwell on God's nature. Think about the infinite ways and means of God! Mentally rehearse what you know to be true about him. For example: *God is love. God is all-powerful. God is ever present. God is all-knowing. God is absolute truth. God is holy. God is merciful. God is faithful. God is just. God is unchanging.* This partial description certainly gives us enough clues to contemplate the perfect character of our Creator.

Praise him in your thoughts:

I praise you, Father God, for being the creator, designer, and architect of the universe. Thank you for the sun, the moon, the stars, and all the planets. I praise you for creating them all. Thank you for being my creator and for creating me in *your* image and likeness. I praise you for the magnificence, simplicity, and brilliance of your creation. The power and sophistication of the human brain is unfathomable. The intricacy and synchronicity of the human body— all its organs, systems, bones, tissues, vessels, and especially its capability to heal and renew itself are utterly remarkable . . .

I praise you for being all-loving. You are not just loving, but love itself. Thank you that when I dwell in love, I dwell in you and *you* in me. I praise you that there is no fear in love. Wherever you are, there also is pure and perfect love. I praise you for your unconditional and unqualified love. Thank you for loving me first. Thank you for knowing everything about me and loving me anyway. Thank you for knowing the worst about me but seeing the best. I praise you for loving me at my worst and loving me at my best. Your love is patient and kind and endures forever, and I am grateful that there will never be a time or place where your everlasting love is not real and powerful and palpable . . .

Lose yourself in God's splendor. Repetition is great. Rambling is fine. Get captivated with his majesty.

Communicate. Remember, he is the vine and we are the branches. If you're a branch, can anything good ever come if you get cut off from the vine? To experience his presence and power, we must stay connected to him. It is our responsibility to initiate and maintain this life link despite our hectic schedules. As described by Kerry and Chris Shook in their wonderful book *One Month to Live*, we accomplish this through continual conversation and confession.

Instead of relegating communication to a single daily prayer time, pray continually throughout the day. These prayers can be casual and conversational, as though talking with a cherished friend. Priority number one is to come clean about your sins right away. Own up to your poor choices immediately. Become a "serial repenter." Never let sins or sorrows accumulate; instead, unload your blunders and burdens to the Lord ASAP.

Next, ask him for help all day long. Invite his feedback.

Seek his direction on both the routine and exceptional agenda items of the day. Delivering your biggest business presentation ever? Ask him for insight. Distracted after an argument with your spouse? Ask him for a soft heart. Don't feel like exercising? Ask him for self-discipline. Disturbed after watching the national news? Ask him how you could be part of the solution. He is never too busy to help us navigate life's challenges or celebrate its victories.

Whether acknowledging sin or seeking wisdom, keep a constant dialogue going with the Creator of the universe, who is with you always. In so doing, you stay connected to eternity while remaining fully alive in each moment.

Saturate. Your greatest asset is God working in you and through you, and this is best accomplished by allowing God's Word to abide in you. When you allow God's Word to permanently occupy your heart and mind, it inevitably shapes your attitude and worldview. As the Word dwells within you, you gain the strength and endurance to act as he would have you act, not as our culture would have you act. And, as Jesus says in John 15:7, "If you remain in me and my words remain in you, you may ask for anything you want, and it will be granted!" (NLT).

Plug yourself into his presence and his power. Pour the Word of God into your soul by memorizing and personalizing Scripture verses. This begins the cleansing process of crowding out negative, limiting thoughts and replacing them with the ultrapositive encouragement of God's promises. The antidote to self-absorption is becoming absorbed in the truth of Christ.

I recommend memorizing one verse per week for the rest of your life. Put yourself into the pages of the Bible by inserting your name and the pronouns *I, me,* and *mine* into your favorite inspirational verses. This technique will help you take ownership of the abundance of spiritual gems that God has laid out for you in the pages of the Bible. Here are some examples of how I personalize Scripture:

- Christ has come so that I, Tommy Newberry, might have life, and have it more abundantly. (See John 10:10, NKJV.)
- God has not given me a spirit of fear, but of power and of love and of a sound mind. (See 2 Timothy 1:7, NKJV.)
- God is my refuge and strength, an ever-present help in trouble. (See Psalm 46:1, NIV.)

Relentlessly rereading the Psalms is an extension of this immersion in Scripture. Slowly ponder the significance of each verse and what God might want to communicate to you through these living words. This kind of meditation is a potent prayer, and you'll find it produces a calm and untroubled mind. Start with revisiting Psalm 23 and then Psalm 91. Then explore everything else and pick a few favorites to memorize, even though they are a bit lengthy. No rush and no worries, though; even the attempt to memorize is a soothing blessing in itself.

Our insatiable appetite for the unhealthy lures of this world diminishes in proportion to our practice of God's presence. With his presence we are satisfied. Without it, nothing can satisfy us. There is no surrogate for God Almighty. Money is not. An exotic vacation is not. The latest popular gadget is not. Food is not. Drugs are not. Alcohol is not. Sex is not. Intelligence is not. Academia is not. Entertainment is not. Nostalgia is not.

While these things may temporarily anesthetize our true longings, they often crowd out God's presence and predictably leave us with only vacant feelings once they wear off. Of course, nothing is inherently wrong with material possessions or external things. But if we worship these things with disproportionate attention and affection, it is easy to feel disconnected from his presence. How we organize our mental priorities makes a massive difference. Only when we escape into his presence can we experience permanent fulfillment.

Indulging in God tames unhealthy cravings and curbs the need to overindulge in food, drink, television, and other temptations of the senses that defer the relationship we crave the most. Nothing gives us rest, peace, and confidence like basking in his presence. The more we practice his presence, the more natural it becomes for us to experience the world through the lens of Philippians 4:8.

And joy is the result.

ACTIVATE 4:8

Drill #40

In today's drill, craft your own miniplan for experiencing God's presence at a deeper level. Borrowing the ideas from this lesson or incorporating your own, in the first column on the following page identify four spiritual habits that will strengthen your daily connection to the Vine. Then, in the next two columns, clarify why each habit is worthwhile and note the first step to implementing the habit in your life.

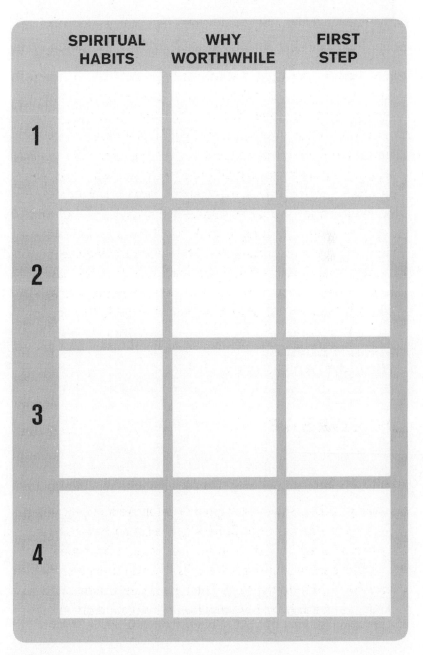

	SPIRITUAL HABITS	WHY WORTHWHILE	FIRST STEP
1			
2			
3			
4			

The Extra Mile

Write a brief note to God, first thanking him for some of your specific blessings. Then ask him to reveal to you any areas of entrenched negativity or unrighteous thinking that may be limiting your capacity to experience his presence at the next level. Date this note for future reference.

_____

_____

_____

_____

_____

Make It Stick:
Thought of the Day

He is here, right now, waiting for me!

Prayer

Heavenly Father, thank you for being my refuge and my strength, closer than the very air I breathe. Prompt me throughout this day and forever to reach for you in my thoughts. Amen.

Notes

DAY 1: Think This, Not That

1. James Allen, in *The Wisdom of James Allen,* ed. Andy Zubko (San Diego, CA: Dove Foundation, 2007), 25.

DAY 9: Take a Vacation from Yourself

2. "The Henry D. Thoreau Quotation Page: Observation," *The Walden Woods Project,* http://www.walden.org/Library/Quotations /Observation.

DAY 22: We Are Sponges

3. James Allen, in *The Wisdom of James Allen,* ed. Andy Zubko, 31.

DAY 27: Don't Sweat the Big Stuff, Either

4. James Allen, in *The Wisdom of James Allen,* ed. Andy Zubko, 25.

DAY 31: Motion Rules Emotion

5. William James, *Talks to Teachers on Psychology: And to Students on Some of Life's Ideals* (Charleston: BiblioBazaar, 2007), 122.

DAY 35: God Will Be Cheering!

6. Tommy Newberry, *Success Is Not an Accident* (Carol Stream, IL: Tyndale House, 2007), 34.

About the Author

TOMMY NEWBERRY is the founder and head coach of The 1% Club, a life-coaching firm that serves entrepreneurs and their families. As a pioneer in the coaching business, he has worked with more than a thousand business leaders in more than thirty industries since 1991.

Tommy's focus is helping entrepreneurs rethink their work so they can achieve their financial goals without compromising their faith, health, and family priorities.

He is the author of several books, including the *New York Times* bestseller *The 4:8 Principle* and the motivational classic, *Success Is Not an Accident,* both of which have been translated into multiple languages.

Tommy has appeared on more than 200 radio and television programs and regularly speaks at business conferences, schools, and churches. He lives in Atlanta with his wife, Kristin, and their three boys. Connect at tommynewberry.com and joychallenge.com.

DISCOVER THE SECRET TO A JOY-FILLED LIFE!

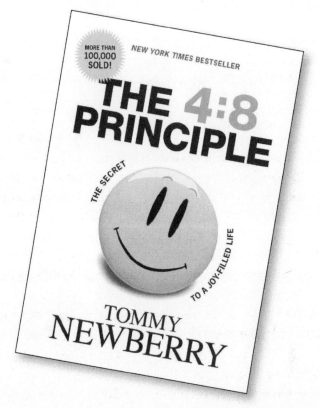

Want to live a happier, healthier, more successful life?

Here's the good news: It's all within your grasp—
and it's easier than you think.

Unlock the power of *The 4:8 Principle* today.
It will forever change the way you think and live!

Now available in stores and online.

By Tommy Newberry

BOOKS

The 4:8 Principle

Success Is Not an Accident

I Call Shotgun

40 Days to a Joy-Filled Life

Think 4:8

For more resources, visit Tommy Newberry
online at tommynewberry.com

CP0114